DR. MONTESSORI'S OWN HANDBOOK

MARIA MONTESSORI

DOVER PUBLICATIONS, INC.
Mineola, New York

Bibliographical Note

This Dover edition, first published in 2005, is an unabridged republication of the work first published in English by William Heinemann, London, in 1914. The color plate originally facing page 46 has been moved to the inside back cover.

International Standard Book Number

ISBN-13: 978-0-486-44525-0
ISBN-10: 0-486-44525-9

Manufactured in the United States by Courier Corporation
44525903
www.doverpublications.com

NOTE BY THE AUTHOR

As a result of the widespread interest that has been taken in my method of child education, certain books have been issued, which may appear to the general reader to be authoritative expositions of the Montessori system. I wish to state definitely that the present work, the English translation of which has been authorised and approved by me, is the only authentic manual of the Montessori method, and that the only other authentic or authorised works of mine in the English language are "The Montessori Method," and "Pedagogical Anthropology.'

Maria Montessori

PREFACE

IF a preface is a light which should serve to illumine the contents of a volume, I choose, not words, but human figures to illustrate this little book intended to enter families where children are growing up. I therefore recall here, as an eloquent symbol, Helen Keller and Mrs. Macy Sullivan, who are, by their example, both teachers to myself—and, before the world, living documents of the miracle in education.

In fact, Helen Keller is a marvellous example of the phenomenon common to all human beings: the possibility of the liberation of the imprisoned spirit of man by the education of the senses. Here lies the basis of the method of education of which the book gives a succinct idea.

If one only of the senses sufficed to make of Helen Keller a woman of exceptional culture and a writer, who better than she proves the potency of that method of education which builds on the senses? If Helen Keller attained through exquisite natural gifts to an elevated conception of the world, who better than she proves that in the inmost self of man lies the spirit ready to reveal itself?

Helen, clasp to your heart these little children, since they, above all others, will understand you. They are your younger brothers: when, with bandaged eyes and in silence, they touch with their little hands, profound impressions rise in their consciousness, and they exclaim with a new form of happiness: " I see with my hands." They alone, then, can fully understand the drama of the mysterious privilege your soul has known. When in darkness and in silence, their spirit left free to expand, their intellectual energy redoubled, they become able to read and write without having learnt, almost as it were by intuition, they, only they, can understand in part the ecstasy which God granted you on the luminous path of learning.

MARIA MONTESSORI.

DR. MONTESSORI'S OWN HANDBOOK

RECENT years have seen a remarkable improvement in the conditions of child life. In all civilised countries, but especially in England, statistics show a decrease in infant mortality.

Related to this decrease in mortality a corresponding improvement is to be seen in the physical development of children; they are physically finer and more vigorous. It has been the diffusion, the popularisation of science, which has brought about such notable advantages. Mothers have learned to welcome the dictates of modern hygiene and to put them into practice in bringing up their children. Many new social institutions have sprung up and have become perfected with the object of assisting children and protecting them during the period of physical growth.

In this way what is practically a new race is coming into being, a race more highly developed, finer and more robust; a race which will be capable of offering resistance to insidious disease.

What has science done to effect this? Science has suggested for us certain very simple rules by which the child has been restored as nearly as possible to conditions of a natural life, and an order and a guiding law have been given to the functions of the body. For example, it is science which suggested maternal feeding, the abolition of swaddling clothes, baths, life in the open air, exercise, simple short clothing, quiet, and plenty of sleep. Rules were also laid down for the measurement of food, adapting it rationally to the physiological needs of the child's life.

Yet with all this, science made no contribution that was entirely new. Mothers had always nursed their children; children had always been clothed; they had breathed and eaten before.

The point is, that the same physical acts which, performed blindly and without order, led to disease and death, when ordered *rationally* were the means of giving strength and life.

The great progress made may perhaps deceive us into thinking that "everything possible" has been done for children.

We have only to weigh the matter carefully, however, to reflect : Are our children only those healthy little bodies which to-day are growing and developing so vigorously under our eyes ? Is their destiny fulfilled in the production of beautiful human bodies ? In that case there would be little difference between their lot and that of the animals which we raise in order to have good meat or beasts of burden.

Man's destiny is evidently other than this, and the care due to the child covers a field wider than that which is considered by physical hygiene. The mother who has given her child his bath and sent him in his perambulator to the park has not fulfilled the mission of the "mother of humanity." The hen which gathers her chickens together, and the cat which licks her kittens and lavishes on them such tender care, differ in no wise from the human mother in the services they render.

No, the human mother if reduced to such limits devotes herself in vain, feels that a higher aspiration has been stifled within her. She is not yet the mother of man. Children must " grow" not only in the body but in the spirit, and the mother longs to follow the mysterious spiritual journey of the beloved one who to-morrow will be the intelligent, divine creation, man.

Science, evidently, has not finished its work. On the contrary, it has scarcely taken the first step in advance, for it has hitherto stopped at the welfare of the body. It must continue, however, to advance : on the same positive lines along which it has improved the health and saved the physical life of the children, it is bound in the future to benefit and to reinforce their inner life, which is the real *human life*. On the same positive lines science will proceed to direct the development of the intelligence, of character, and of those latent creative forces which lie hidden in the marvellous embryo of man's spirit.

As the child's body must draw nourishment and oxygen from its external environment, in order to accomplish a great physiological work, the *work of growth*, so also the spirit must take from its environment the nourishment which it needs to develop according to its own " laws of growth." It cannot be denied that the phenomena of development are a great work in themselves. The consolidation of the bones, the growth of the whole body, the completion of the minute construction of the brain, the formation of the teeth, all these are very real labours of the physiological organism, as is also the transformation which the organism undergoes during the period of puberty.

Such exertions are very different from those put forth by mankind in so-called *external work*, that is to say, in " social production," whether in the schools where man is taught, or in the world where, by the activity of his intelligence, he produces wealth and transforms his environment.

It is none the less true, however, that they are both " work." In fact, the organism during these periods of greatest physiological work is least capable of performing external tasks, and sometimes the work of growth is of such extent and difficulty that the individual is overburdened, as with an excessive strain, and for this reason alone becomes exhausted, or even dies.

Man will always be able to avoid " external work " by making use of the labour of others, but there is no possibility of shirking that inner work. Together with birth and death it has been imposed by nature itself, and each man must accomplish it for himself. This difficult, inevitable labour, —this is the " work of the child."

When we say then that little children should *rest*, we are referring to one side only of the question of work. We mean that they should rest from that *external* visible work to which the little child through his weakness and incapacity cannot make any contribution useful either to himself or to others.

Our assertion, therefore, is not absolute; the child in reality is not "resting," he is performing the mysterious inner work of his autoformation. He is working to make a man, and to accomplish this it is not enough that the child's body should grow in actual size; the most intimate functions of the motor and nervous systems must also be established, and the intelligence developed.

The functions to be established by the child fall into two groups: (1) the motor functions by which he is to secure his balance and learn to walk, and to co-ordinate his movements; (2) the sensory functions through which, receiving sensations from his environment, he lays the foundations of his intelligence by a continual exercise of observation, comparison and judgment. In this way he gradually comes to be acquainted with his environment and to develop his intelligence.

At the same time he is learning a *language*, and

he is faced not only with the motor difficulties of articulation, sounds and words, but also with the difficulty of gaining an intelligent understanding of names and of the syntactical composition of the language.

If we think of an emigrant who goes to a new, country ignorant of its products, ignorant of its natural appearance and social order, entirely ignorant of its language, we realise that there is an immense work of adaptation which he must perform before he can associate himself with the active life of the unknown people. No one will be able to do for him that work of adaptation. He himself must observe, understand, remember, form judgments, and learn the new language by laborious exercise and long experience.

What is to be said then of the child? What of this emigrant who comes into a new world, and who, weak as he is and before his organism is completely developed, *must* in a short time adapt himself to a world so complex?

Up to the present day the little child has not received rational aid in the accomplishment of this laborious task. As regards the psychical development of the child we find ourselves in a period parallel to that in which the physical life was left to the mercy of chance and instinct—the period in which infant mortality was a scourge.

It is by scientific and rational means also that we must facilitate that inner work of psychical adaptation to be accomplished within the child, a work which is by no means the same thing as any external work or production whatsoever.

This is the aim which underlies my method of infant education, and it is for this reason that certain principles which it enunciates, together with that part which deals with the technique of their practical application, are not of a general character, but have special reference to the particular case of the child from three to seven years of age, *i.e.*, to the needs of a formative period of life.

My method is scientific, both in its substance and in its aim. It makes for the attainment of a more advanced stage of progress, in directions no longer only material and physiological. It is an endeavour to complete the course which hygiene has already taken, but in the treatment of the physical side alone.

If to-day we possessed statistics respecting the nervous debility, defects of speech, errors of perception and of reasoning, and lack of character in normal children, it would perhaps be interesting to compare them with statistics of the same nature, but compiled from the study of children who have had a number of years of rational education. In all probability we should find a striking resemblance between such statistics and those to-day available showing the decrease in mortality and the improvement in the physical development of children.

A " CHILDREN'S HOUSE "

The " Children's House" is the *environment* which is offered to the child that he may be given the opportunity of developing his activities. This kind of school is not of a fixed type, but may vary according to the financial resources at disposal and to the opportunities afforded by the environment. It ought to be a real house ; that is to say, a set of rooms with a garden of which the children are the masters. A garden which contains shelters is ideal, because the children can play or sleep under them, and can also bring their tables out to work or dine. In this way they may live almost entirely in the open air, and are protected at the same time from rain and sun.

The central and principal room of the building, often also the only room at the disposal of the children, is the room for "intellectual work." To this central room can be added other smaller rooms according to the means and opportunities of the place: for example, a bath-room, a dining-room, a little parlour or common-room, a room for manual work, a gymnasium and rest-room.

The special characteristic of the equipment of these houses is that it is adapted for children and not adults. They contain not only a didactic material specially fitted for the intellectual development of the child, but also a complete equipment for the management of the miniature family. The furniture is light so that the children can move it about, and it is painted in some light colour so that the children can wash it with soap and water. There are small tables of various sizes and shapes—square, rectangular and round, large and small. The rectangular shape is the most common as two or more children can work at it together. The seats are small wooden chairs, but there are also small wicker armchairs and sofas.

In the working-room there are two indispensable pieces of furniture. One of these is a very long cupboard with large doors (Fig. 1). It is very low so that a small child can set on the top of it small objects such as mats, flowers, etc. Inside this cupboard is kept the didactic material which is the common property of all the children.

FIG. 1.—CUPBOARD WITH APPARATUS.

The other is a chest of drawers containing two or three columns of little drawers, each of which has a bright handle (or a handle of some colour to contrast with the background), and a small card with a name upon it. Every child has his own drawer, in which to put things belonging to him.

Round the walls of the room are fixed black-boards at a low level, so that the children can write or draw on them, and pleasing, artistic pictures, which are changed from time to time as circumstances direct.   The pictures represent children, families, landscapes, flowers and fruit, and more often Biblical and historical incidents. Ornamental plants and flowering plants ought always to be placed in the room where the children are at work.

Another part of the working-room's equipment is seen in the pieces of carpet of various colours— red, blue, pink, green and brown.   The children spread these rugs upon the floor, sit upon them and work there with the didactic material.   A room of this kind is larger than the customary class-rooms, not only because the little tables and separate chairs take up more space, but also because a large part of the floor must be free for the children to spread their rugs and work upon them.

In the sitting-room, or " club-room," a kind of parlour in which the children amuse themselves by conversation, games, or music, etc., the furnish-ings should be especially tasteful.   Little tables of different sizes, little arm-chairs and sofas should

be placed here and there. Many brackets of all
kinds and sizes, upon which may be put statuettes
artistic vases or framed photographs, should adorn
the walls ; and, above all, each child should have
a little flower-pot, in which he may sow the seed
of some indoor plant, to tend and cultivate as it
grows. On the tables of this sitting-room should
be placed large albums of coloured pictures, and
also games of patience, or various geometric solids,
with which the children can play at pleasure,
constructing figures, etc. A piano, or better, other
musical instruments, possibly harps of small
dimensions, made especially for children, complete
the equipment. In this " club-room " the teacher
may sometimes entertain the children with stories,
which will attract a circle of interested listeners.

The furniture of the dining-room consists, in
addition to the tables, of low cupboards accessible
to all the children, who can themselves put in their
place and take away the crockery, spoons, knives
and forks, table-cloth and napkins. The plates
are always of china, and the tumblers and water-
bottles of glass. Knives are always included in
the table equipment.

The Dressing-room. Here each child has his
own little cupboard or shelf. In the middle of

the room there are very simple washhand-stands, consisting of tables, on each of which stand a small basin, soap and nail-bush. Against the wall stand little sinks with water-taps. Here the children may draw and pour away their water. There is nothing to limit the equipment of the "Children's Houses" because the children themselves do everything. They sweep the rooms, dust and wash the furniture, polish the brasses, lay and clear away the table, wash up, sweep and roll up the rugs, wash a few little clothes, and cook eggs. As regards their personal toilet, the children know how to dress and undress themselves. They hang their clothes on little hooks, placed very low so as to be within reach of a little child, or else they fold up such articles of clothing, as their little serving-aprons, of which they take great care, and lay them inside a cupboard kept for the household linen.

In short, where the manufacture of toys has been brought to such a point of complication and perfection that children have at their disposal entire dolls' houses, complete wardrobes for the dressing and undressing of dolls, kitchens where they can pretend to cook, toy animals as nearly lifelike as possible, this method seeks to give all this to the child in reality—making him an actor in a living scene.

My *pœdometer* forms part of the equipment of a "Children's House." After various modifications I have now reduced this instrument to a very practical form (Fig. 2).

The purpose of the pædometer, as its name shows, is to measure the children. It consists of a wide rectangular board, forming the base, from the centre of which rise two wooden posts held together at the top by a narrow flat piece of metal. To each post is connected a horizontal

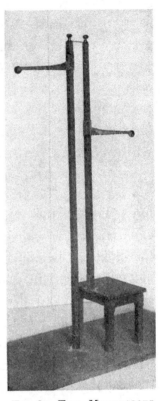

FIG. 2.—THE MONTESSORI PÆDOMETER.

metal rod—the indicator—which runs up and down by means of a casing, also of metal. This metal casing is made in one piece with the indicator, to the end of which is fixed an india-rubber ball. On one side, that is to say, behind one of the two tall vertical wooden posts, there is a small seat, also of wood. The two tall wooden posts are graduated. The post to which the seat is fixed is graduated from the surface of the seat to the top, whilst the other is graduated from the wooden board at the base to the top, *i.e.* to a height of 1·50 metres. On the side containing the seat the height of the child seated is measured, on the other side the child's full stature. The practical value of this instrument lies in the possibility of measuring two children at the same time, and in the fact that the children themselves co-operate in taking the measurements. In fact, they learn to take off their shoes and to place themselves in the correct position on the pædometer. They find no difficulty in raising and lowering the metal indicators, which are held so firmly in place by means of the metal casing that they cannot deviate from their horizontal position even when used by inexpert hands. Moreover, they run extremely easily, so that very little strength is required to move them. The little indiarubber balls prevent the children from hurting themselves should they inadvertently knock their heads against the metal indicator.

The children are very fond of the pædometer. " Shall we measure ourselves ? " is one of the proposals which they make most willingly and with the greatest likelihood of finding many of their companions to join them. They also take great care of the pædometer, dusting it, and polishing its metal parts. All the surfaces of the pædometer, in addition to the metal, are so smooth and well polished that they invite the care that is taken of them, and by their appearance when finished fully repay the trouble taken.

The pædometer represents the scientific part of the method, because it has reference to the anthropological and psychological study made of the children, each of whom has his own bio-graphical record. This biographical record follows the history of the child's development according to the observations which it is possible to make by the application of my method. This subject is dealt with at length in my other books. A series of cinematograph pictures has been taken of the pædometer at a moment when the children are being measured. They are seen coming of their own accord, even the very smallest, to take their places at the instrument.

THE METHOD

The technique of my method, as it follows the guidance of the natural physiological and psychical development of the child, may be divided into three parts :

Motor education.
Sensory education.
Language.

The care and management of the environment itself afford the principal means of motor education; while sensory education and the education of language are provided for by my didactic material.

The didactic material for the *education of the senses* consists of :—

(*a*) Three sets of solid insets.
(*b*) Three sets of solids in graduated sizes, comprising—
    (1) Pink cubes.
    (2) Brown prisms.
    (3) Rods : (*a*) coloured green ; (*b*) coloured alternately red and blue.

(c) Various geometric solids (prism, pyramid, sphere, cylinder, cone, etc.).

(d) Rectangular tablets with rough and smooth surfaces.

(e) A collection of various stuffs.

(f) Small wooden tablets of different weights.

(g) Two boxes, each containing sixty-four coloured tablets.

(h) A chest of drawers containing plane insets.

(i) Three series of cards on which are pasted geometrical forms in paper.

(k) A collection of cylindrical closed boxes (sounds).

(l) A double series of musical bells ; wooden boards on which are painted the lines used in music ; small wooden discs for the notes.

Didactic Material for the Preparation for Writing and Arithmetic

(m) Two sloping desks and various iron insets.

(n) Cards on which are pasted sandpaper letters.

(o) Two alphabets of coloured cardboard and of different sizes.

(p) A series of cards on which are pasted sandpaper figures (1, 2, 3, etc.).

(*q*) A series of large cards bearing the same figures in smooth paper for the enumeration of numbers above ten.

(*r*) Two boxes with small sticks for counting.

(*s*) The volume of drawings belonging specially to the method, and coloured pencils.

(*t*) The frames for lacing, buttoning, etc., which are used for motor education of the hand.

MOTOR EDUCATION

The education of the movements is very complex, as it must correspond to all the co-ordinated movements which the child has to establish in his physiological organism. The child, if left without guidance, is disorderly in his movements, and these disorderly movements are the *special characteristic of the little child.* In fact, he " never keeps still," and " touches everything." This is what forms the child's so-called " unruliness " and " naughtiness."

The adult would deal with him by checking these movements, with the monotonous and useless repetition " keep still." As a matter of fact, in these movements the little one is seeking the very exercise which will organise and co-ordinate the movements useful to man. We must therefore desist from the useless attempt to reduce the child to a state of immobility. We should rather give " order " to his movements, leading him to those actions towards which his efforts are actually tending. This is the aim of muscular education at this age. Once a direction is given to them, the child's movements are made towards a definite end, so that he himself grows quiet and contented, and becomes an active worker, a being calm and full of joy. This education of the movements is one of the principal factors in producing that outward appearance of " discipline " to be found in the Children's Houses. I have already spoken at length on this subject in my other books.

Muscular education has reference:

To the primary movements of everyday life (walking, rising, sitting, handling objects).

The care of the person.

Management of the household.

Gardening.

Manual work.

The gymnasium.

Rhythmic movements.

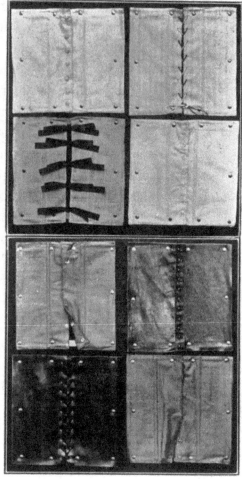

FIG. 3.—FRAMES FOR LACING AND BUTTONING.

In the care of the person the first step is that of dressing and undressing. For this end there is in my didactic material a collection of frames to which are attached pieces of stuff, leather, etc.

These can be buttoned, hooked, tied together — in fact, joined in all the different ways which our civilisation has invented for fastening our clothing, shoes, etc. (Fig. 3).

The teacher, sitting down by the child's side, performs the necessary movements of the fingers very slowly and deliberately, separating the movements themselves

FIG. 4.—CHILD BUTTONING ON FRAME. (Photo taken at Mr. Hawker's School at Runton.)

into their different parts, and letting them be seen clearly and minutely.

For example, one of the first actions will be the adjustment of the two pieces of stuff in such a way that the edges to be fastened together touch one another from top to bottom. Then if it is a buttoning-frame, the teacher will show the child the different stages of the action. She will take hold of the button, set it opposite the button-hole, make it enter the buttonhole completely, and adjust it carefully in its place above. In the same way, to teach a child to tie a bow, she will separate the stage in which he ties the ribbons together from that in which he makes the bows.

In the cinematograph film there is a picture which shows an entire lesson in the tying of the bows with the ribbons. These lessons are not necessary for all the children, as they learn from one another, and of their own accord come with great patience to analyse the movements, performing them separately very slowly and carefully. The child can sit in a comfortable position and hold his frame on the table (Fig. 4). As he fastens and unfastens the same frame many times over with great interest, he acquires an unusual deftness of hand, and becomes possessed with the desire to fasten real clothes whenever he has the opportunity. We see the smallest children *wanting* to dress themselves and their companions. They go in search of amusement of this kind, and defend themselves with all their might against the adult who would try to help them.

In the same way for the teaching of the other and larger movements, such as washing, setting the table, etc., the directress must at the beginning intervene, teaching the child with few or no words at all, but with very precise actions. She teaches all the movements; how to sit, to rise from one's seat, to take up and lay down objects, and to offer them gracefully to others. In the same way she teaches the children to set the plates one upon the other and lay them on the table without making any noise, etc.

The children learn easily and show an interest and a surprising care in the performance of these actions. In classes where there are many children it is necessary to arrange for the children to take turns in the various household duties, such as doing the housework, serving at table, washing the dishes, etc. The children readily respect such a system of turns. There is no need to ask them to do this work, for they come spontaneously— even little ones of two and a half years old—to offer themselves, and it is frequently most touching to watch their efforts to imitate, to remember, and, finally, to conquer their difficulty. Professor Jacoby, of New York, was once much moved as he watched a child, who was little more than two

years old and not at all intelligent in appearance,
standing perplexed, because he could not remember
whether the fork should be set at the right hand
or the left. He remained a long while meditating
and evidently using all the powers of his mind.
The other children older than he watched him
with admiration, marvelling, like ourselves, at the
life developing under our eyes.

The instructions of the teacher consist then
merely in a hint, a touch—enough to give a start
to the child. The rest develops of itself. The
children learn from one another and throw themselves into the work with enthusiasm and delight.
This atmosphere of quiet activity develops a
fellow-feeling, an attitude of mutual aid, and,
most wonderful of all, an intelligent interest on
the part of the older children in the progress of
their little companions. It is enough just to set
a child in these peaceful surroundings for him to
feel perfectly at home. In the cinematograph
pictures the actual work in a Children's House
may be seen. The children are moving about,
each one fulfilling his own task, whilst the
teacher is in a corner watching. Pictures were
also taken of the children engaged in the care of
the house, that is, in the care both of their

persons and their surroundings. They can be seen washing their faces, polishing their shoes, washing the furniture, polishing the metal indicators of the pædometer, brushing the carpets, etc. In the work of laying the table the children are seen quite by themselves, dividing the work among themselves, carrying the plates, spoons, forks and knives, etc., and, finally, sitting down at the tables where the little waitresses serve the hot soup.

Again, gardening and manual work are a great pleasure to our children. Gardening is already well known as a feature of infant education, and it is recognised by all that plants and animals attract the children's care and attention. The ideal of the Children's Houses in this respect is to imitate the best in the present usage of those schools, which owe their inspiration more or less to Mrs. Latter.

For manual instruction we have chosen clay work, consisting of the construction of little tiles, vases and bricks. These may be made with the help of simple instruments, such as moulds. The *completion* of the work should be the aim always kept in view, and, finally, all the little objects made by the children should be glazed and baked in the furnace. The children themselves learn to line a wall with shining white or coloured tiles wrought in various designs, or, with the help of mortar and a trowel, to cover the floor with little bricks. They also dig out foundations and then use their bricks to build division walls, or entire little houses for the chickens.

Among the gymnastic exercises that which must be considered the most important is that of the " line." A line is described in chalk or paint upon a large space of floor. Instead of one line, there may also be two concentric lines, elliptical in form. The children are taught to walk upon these lines like tight-rope walkers, placing their feet one in front of the other. To keep their balance they make efforts exactly similar to those of real tight-rope walkers, except that they have no danger with which to reckon, as the lines are only *drawn* upon the floor. The teacher herself performs the exercise, showing clearly how she sets her feet, and the children imitate her without any necessity for her to speak. At first it is only certain children who follow her, and when she has shown them how to do it, she withdraws, leaving the phenomenon to develop of itself.

The children for the most part continue to walk,

adapting their feet with great care to the movement they have seen, and making efforts to keep
their balance so as not to fall. Gradually the
other children draw near and watch and also
make an attempt. Very little time elapses before
the whole of the two ellipses or the one line is
covered with children balancing themselves, and
continuing to walk round, watching their feet
with an expression of deep attention · on their
faces.

Music may then be used. It should be a very
simple march, the rhythm of which is not obvious
at first, but which accompanies and enlivens the
spontaneous efforts of the children.

When they have learned in this way to master
their balance the children have brought the act
of walking to a remarkable standard of perfection,
and have acquired, in addition to security and
composure in their natural gait, an unusually
graceful carriage of the body. The exercise on
the line can afterwards be made more complicated
in various ways. The first application is that of
calling forth rhythmic exercise by the sound of a
march upon the piano. When the same march
is repeated during several days, the children end
by feeling the rhythm and by following it with

movements of their arms and feet. They also accompany the exercises on the line with songs.

Little by little the music is *understood* by the children. They finish, as in Miss George's school at Washington, by singing over their daily work with the didactic material. The Children's House, then, resembles a hive of bees humming as they work.

As to the little gymnasium, of which I speak in my book on the " Method," one piece of apparatus is particularly practical. This is the " fence," from which the children hang by the arms, freeing their legs from the heavy weight of the body and strengthening the arms. This fence also has the advantage of being useful in a garden for the purpose of dividing one part from another, as, for example, the flower beds from the garden walks, and it does not detract in any way from the appearance of the garden.

SENSORY EDUCATION

My didactic material offers to the child the *means* for what may be called " sensory education."

In the box of material the first three objects which are likely to attract the attention of a little child from two and a half to three years

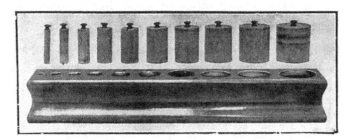

FIG. 5.—CYLINDERS DECREASING IN DIAMETER ONLY.

FIG. 6.—CYLINDERS DECREASING IN DIAMETER AND HEIGHT.

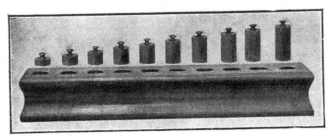

FIG. 7.—CYLINDERS DECREASING IN HEIGHT ONLY.

old are three solid pieces of wood, in each of which
is inserted a row of ten small cylinders, or
sometimes discs, all furnished with a button for
a handle. In the first case there is a row of
cylinders of the same height, but with a
diameter which decreases from thick to thin
(Fig. 5). In the second there are cylinders, which
decrease in all dimensions, and so are either
larger or smaller, but always of the same shape
(Fig. 6). Lastly, in the third case, the cylinders
have the same diameter but vary in height, so
that, as the size decreases, the cylinder gradually
becomes a little disc in form (Fig. 7).

The first cylinders vary in two dimensions (the
section); the second in all three dimensions;
the third in one dimension (height). The order
which I have given refers to the degree of *ease* with
which the child performs the exercises.

The exercise consists in taking out the cylinders,
mixing them and putting them back in the right
place. It is performed by the child as he sits
in a comfortable position at a little table. He
exercises his hands in the delicate act of taking
hold of the button with the tips of one or two
fingers, and in the little movements of the hand
and arm as he mixes the cylinders, *without letting*

them fall and *without making too much noise* and puts them back again each in its own place.

In these exercises the teacher may, in the first instance, intervene, merely taking out the cylinders, mixing them carefully on the table and then showing the child that he is to put them back, but without performing the action herself. Such intervention, however, is almost always found to be unnecessary, for the children *see* their companions at work, and thus are encouraged to imitate them. They like to do it *alone ;* in fact, some-

Fig. 8.—Child using Case of Cylinders.

times almost in private for fear of inopportune help (Fig. 8).

But how is the child to find the right place for each of the little cylinders which lie mixed upon the table ? He first makes trials ; it often happens that he places a cylinder which is too large for the empty hole over which he places it. Then, changing its place, he tries others until the cylinder goes in. Again, the contrary may happen ; that is to say, the cylinder may slip too easily into a hole too big for it. In that case it has taken a place which does not belong to it at all, but to a larger cylinder. In this way one cylinder at the end will be left out without a place, and it will not be possible to find one that fits. Here the child cannot help seeing his mistake in concrete form. He is perplexed, his little mind is faced with a problem which interests him intensely. Before, all the cylinders fitted, now there is one that will not fit. The little one stops, frowning, deep in thought. He begins to feel the little buttons and finds that some cylinders have too much room. He thinks that perhaps they are out of their right place and tries to place them correctly. He repeats the process again and again, and finally he succeeds. Then it is that he breaks into a smile of triumph. The exercise arouses the intelligence of the child ; he wants to repeat it right from the beginning and, having learned by experience, he makes another attempt. Little children from three to three and a half years old have repeated the exercise up to *forty* times without losing their interest in it.

If the second set of cylinders and then the third are presented, the *change* of shape strikes the child and reawakens his interest.

The material which I have described serves to *educate the eye* to distinguish *difference in dimension,* for the child ends by being able to recognise at a glance the larger or the smaller hole which exactly fits the cylinder which he holds in his hand. The educative process is based on this : that the control of the error lies in *the material itself,* and the child has concrete evidence of it.

The desire of the child to attain an end which he knows leads him to correct himself. It is not therefore a teacher who

FIG. 9.—THE TOWER.

makes him notice his mistake and shows him how to correct it, but it is a complex work of the child's own intelligence which leads to such a result.

Hence at this point there begins the process of auto-education. The aim is not an external one, that is to say, it is *not* the object that the child should learn how to place the cylinders, and *that he should know how to perform an exercise.* The

Fig. 10.—Child Playing with Tower. (Photo taken at Mr. Hawker's School at Runton.)

aim is an inner one, namely, that the child train himself to observe ; that he be led to make comparisons between objects, to form judgments, to reason and to decide ; and it is in the indefinite repetition of this exercise of attention and of intelligence that a real development ensues.

The series of objects to follow after the

FIG. 11.—THE BROAD STAIR.

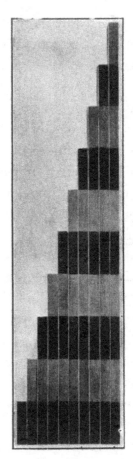

FIG. 12.—THE LONG STAIR.

cylinders consist of three sets of geometrical solid forms :

(1) Ten wooden cubes coloured pink. The sides of the cubes diminish from ten centimetres to one centimetre (Fig. 9).

With these cubes the child builds a tower, first laying on the ground (upon a carpet) the largest cube, and then placing on the top of it all the others in their order of size to the very smallest (Fig. 10).   As soon as he has built the tower, the child, with a blow of his hand, knocks it down, so that the cubes are scattered on the carpet, and then he builds it up again.

Another set consists of ten wooden prisms coloured brown. The length of the prisms is twenty centimetres, and the square section diminishes from ten centimetres a side to the smallest, of one centimetre a side (Fig. 11).

The child scatters the ten pieces over a light coloured carpet and then, beginning sometimes with the thickest, sometimes with the thinnest, he places them in their right order of gradation upon a table.

The third set consists of ten rods coloured green, or alternately red and blue, all of which have the same square section of four centimetres a side, but vary by ten centimetres in length from ten centimetres to one metre (Fig. 12).

The child scatters the ten rods on a large carpet and mixes them at random, and, by comparing rod with rod, he arranges them according to their order of length, so that they take the form of a set of organ pipes.

As usual, the teacher, by doing the exercises herself, first shows the child how the pieces of each set should be arranged, but it will often happen that the child learns, not directly from her, but by watching his companions. She will, however, always continue to watch the children, never losing sight of their efforts, and any correction of hers will be directed more towards preventing rough or disorderly use of the material than towards any *error* which the child may make in placing the rods in their order of gradation. The reason is that the mistakes which the child makes, by placing, for example, a small cube beneath one that is larger, are caused by his own lack of education, and it is the *repetition of the exercise* which, by refining his powers of observation, will lead him sooner or later to *correct himself.* Sometimes it happens that a child working with the long rods makes the most glaring mistakes. As the aim of the exercise, however, is *not* that the rods be arranged in the right order of gradation, but that the child *should practise by himself,* there is no need to intervene.

One day the child will arrange all the rods in their right order, and then, full of joy, he will call the teacher to come and admire them. The object of the exercise will thus be achieved.

These three sets, the cubes, the prisms, and the rods, cause the child to move about and to handle and carry objects which are difficult for him to grasp with his little hand. Again, by their use, he repeats the *training of the eye* to the recognition of differences in size between similar objects. The exercise would seem easier, from the sensory point of view, than the other with the cylinders described above.

As a matter of fact, it is more difficult, as there is *no control of the error in the material itself.* It is the child's eye alone which can furnish the control.

Hence the difference between the objects should strike the eye at once ; for that reason larger objects are used, and the necessary visual power presupposes a previous preparation (provided for in the exercise with the solid insets).

During the same period the child can be doing other exercises. Amongst the material is to be found a small rectangular board, the surface of which is divided into two parts—rough and smooth (Fig. 13). The child knows already how to wash his hands with cold water and soap; he then dries them and dips the tips of his fingers for a few seconds in tepid water. Graduated exercises for the thermic sense may also have their place

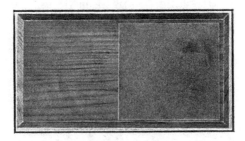

Fig. 13.—Board with Rough and Smooth Surfaces.

here, as has been explained in my book on the method.

After this, the child is taught to pass the soft cushioned tips of his fingers *as lightly as possible* over the two separate surfaces, that he may appreciate their difference. The delicate movement backwards and forwards of the suspended hand, as it is brought into light contact with the surface, is an excellent exercise in control. The little hand, which has just been cleansed and taken its tepid bath, gains much in grace and beauty, and the whole exercise is the first step in the education of the " tactile sense," which holds such an important place in my method.

When initiating the child into the education of the sense of touch, the teacher must always take an active part the first time ; not only must she show the child " how it is done," her inter-

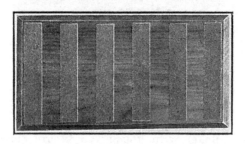

Fig. 14.—Board with Gummed Strips of Paper.

ference is a little more definite still, for she takes hold of his hand and guides it to touch the surfaces with the finger-tips in the lightest possible way.   She will make no explanations ; her words will be rather to *encourage* the child with his hand to perceive the different sensations.   When he has perceived them, it is then that he repeats the act by himself in the delicate way which he has been taught.

After the board with the two contrasting

surfaces, the child is offered another board on which are gummed strips of paper which are rough or smooth in different degrees (Fig. 14).

Graduated series of sandpaper cards are also given. The child perfects himself by exercises in touching these surfaces, not only refining his capacity for perceiving tactile differences which are always growing more similar, but also perfecting the movement of which he is ever gaining greater mastery.

Following these is a series of stuffs of every kind : velvets, satins, silks, woollens, cottons, coarse and fine linens. There are two similar pieces of each kind of stuff, and they are of bright and vivid colours.

The child is now taught a new movement. Where before he had to *touch,* he must now *feel* the stuffs, which, according to the degree of fineness or coarseness from coarse cotton to fine silk, are felt with movements correspondingly decisive or delicate. The child whose hand is already practised finds the greatest pleasure in feeling the stuffs, and, almost instinctively, in order to enhance his appreciation of the tactile sensation he closes his eyes. Then, to spare himself the exertion, he blindfolds himself with a clean handkerchief, and as he feels the stuffs, arranges the similar pieces in pairs, one upon the other. Then, taking off the handkerchief, he ascertains for himself whether he has made any mistake.

This exercise in touching and feeling is peculiarly attractive to the child, and induces him to seek similar experiences in his surroundings. A little one, attracted by the pretty stuff of a visitor's dress, will be seen to go and wash his hands, then to come and touch the stuff of the garment again and again with infinite delicacy, his face meanwhile expressing his pleasure and interest.

A little later we shall see the children interest themselves in a much more difficult exercise. There are some little rectangular tablets which form part of the material (Fig. 15). The tablets, though of identical size, are made of wood of varying qualities, so that they differ in weight and, through the property of the wood, in colour also.

The child has to take a tablet and rest it delicately on the inner surfaces of his four fingers, spreading them well out. This will be another opportunity of teaching delicate movements.

The hand must move up and down as though to weigh the object, but the movement must be

as imperceptible as possible. These little movements should diminish as the capacity and attention for perceiving the weight of the object become
more acute, and the exercise will be perfectly
performed when the child comes to perceive the
weight almost without any movement of the
hands. It is only by the repetition of the
attempts that such a result can be obtained.

FIG. 15.—WOOD TABLETS DIFFERING IN WEIGHT.

Once the children are initiated into it by the
teacher, they blindfold their eyes and repeat by
themselves these exercises of the *baric sense*. For
example, they lay the heavier wooden tablets on
the right and the lighter on the left. When the
child takes off the handkerchief, he can see by
the colour of the pieces of wood if he has made
a mistake.

A long time before this difficult exercise, and

during the period when the child is working with the three sorts of geometrical solids and with the rough and smooth tablets, he can be exercising himself with a material which is very attractive to him.

This is the set of tablets covered with bright silk of shaded colours. The set consists of two separate boxes each containing sixty-four colours ; that is, eight different tints, each of which has eight shades carefully graded. *

The first exercise for the child is that of *pairing the colours ;* that is, he selects from a mixed heap of colours the two tablets which are alike, and lays them out, one beside the other. The teacher naturally does not offer the child all the one hundred and twenty-eight tablets in a heap, but chooses only a few of the brighter colours, for example, red, blue and yellow, and prepares and mixes up three or four pairs. Then, taking one tablet—perhaps the red one—she indicates to the child that he is to choose its counterpart from the heap. This done, the teacher lays the pair together on the table. Then she takes perhaps the blue, and the child selects the tablet to form another pair. The teacher then mixes the tablets again for the child to repeat the exercise by

*Please refer to color plate on inside back cover.

himself, *i.e.*, to select the two red tablets, the two blue, the two yellow, etc., and to place the two members of each pair next to one another.

Then the couples will be increased to four or five, and little children of three years old end by pairing of their own accord ten or a dozen couples of mixed tablets.

When the child has given his eye sufficient practice in recognising the identity of the pairs of colours, he is offered the shades of one colour only, and he exercises himself in the perception of the slightest differences of shade in every colour. Take, for example, the blue series. There are eight tablets in graduated shades. The teacher places them one next another, beginning with the darkest, with the sole object of making the child understand "what is to be done." She then leaves him alone to the interesting attempts which he spontaneously makes.

It often happens that the child makes a mistake. If he has understood the idea and makes a mistake, it is a sign that *he has not yet reached the stage* of perceiving the differences between the graduations of one colour. It is practice which perfects in the child that capacity for distinguishing the fine differences, and so we leave him alone to his attempts. There are two suggestions that we can make to help him. The first is that he should always select the darkest colour from the pile. This suggestion greatly facilitates his choice by giving it a constant direction.

Secondly, we can lead him to observe from time to time any two colours that stand next to one another in order to compare them directly and apart from the others. In this way the child does not place a tablet without a particular and careful comparison with its neighbour.

Finally, the child himself will love to mix the sixty-four colours and then to arrange them in eight rows of pretty shades of colour with really surprising skill. In this exercise also the child's hand is educated to perform fine and delicate movements and his mind is afforded special training in attention. He must not take hold of the tablets anyhow, he must avoid touching the coloured silk, and must handle the tablets instead by the pieces of wood at the top and bottom. To arrange the tablets next to one another in a straight line at exactly the same level, so that the series looks like a beautiful shaded ribbon, is an act which demands a manual skill only obtained after considerable practice.

These exercises of the chromatic sense lead, in the case of the older children, to the development of the " colour memory." A child having looked carefully at a colour, is then invited to look for its companion in a mixed group of colours, without

FIG. 16.—CABINET WITH DRAWERS TO HOLD GEOMETRICAL INSETS.

of course keeping the colour he has observed under his eye to guide him. It is therefore by his memory that he recognises the colour, which he no longer compares with a reality but with an image impressed upon his mind.

The children are very fond of this exercise in " colour memory "; it makes a very lively digression for them, as they run with the image

of a colour in their minds and look for its corresponding reality in their surroundings. It is a
real triumph for them to identify the idea with
the corresponding reality and to *hold in their hands*
the proof of the mental power they have acquired.

FIG. 17.—SET OF SIX CIRCLES.

Another interesting piece of material is a little
cabinet containing six drawers placed one above
another. When they are opened they display six
square wooden " frames " in each (Fig. 16).

Almost all the frames have a large geometrical
figure inserted in the centre, each coloured blue
and provided with a small button for a handle.

Each drawer is lined with blue paper, and when the geometrical figure is removed, the bottom is seen to reproduce exactly the same form.

The geometrical figures are arranged in the drawers according to analogy of form.

FIG. 18.—SET OF SIX RECTANGLES.

(1) In one drawer there are six circles decreasing in diameter (Fig. 17).

(2) In another there is a square, together with five rectangles in which the length is always equal to the side of the square while the breadth gradually decreases (Fig. 18).

(3) Another drawer contains six triangles, which

vary either according to their sides or according to their angles (equilateral, isosceles, scalene, right-angled, obtuse angled, and acute angled) (Fig. 19).

(4) In another drawer there are six regular polygons containing from five to ten sides, *i.e.*,

FIG. 19.—SET OF SIX TRIANGLES.

the pentagon, hexagon, heptagon, octagon, nonagon, and decagon (Fig. 20).

(5) Another drawer contains various figures, an oval, an ellipse, a rhombus, a rhomboid, and a trapezoid (Fig. 21).

(6) Finally, there are four plain wooden tablets, *i.e.*, without any geometrical inset, which should

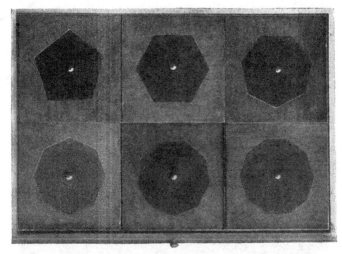

FIG. 20.—SET OF SIX POLYGONS.

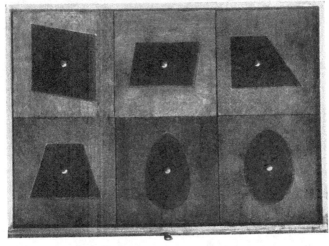

FIG. 21.—SET OF SIX IRREGULAR FIGURES.

have no button fixed to them; also two other irregular geometrical figures (Fig. 22).

Connected with this material there is a wooden frame furnished with a kind of rack which opens like a lid, and serves, when shut, to keep firmly

FIG. 22.—SET OF FOUR BLANKS AND TWO IRREGULAR
FIGURES.

in place six of the insets, which may be arranged on the bottom of the frame itself, entirely covering it (Fig. 23).

This frame is used for the preparation of the *first presentation* to the child of the plane geometrical forms.

The teacher may select according to her own

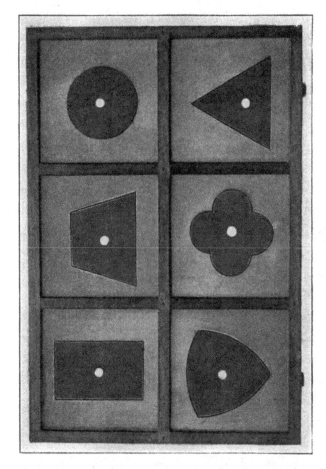

FIG. 23.—FRAME TO HOLD GEOMETRICAL INSETS.

judgment certain forms from amongst the whole series at her disposal.

At first it is advisable to show the child only a few figures which differ very widely from each other in form. The next step is to present a larger number of figures, and after this to present, consecutively, figures more and more similar in form.

The first figures to be arranged in the frame will be, for example, the circle and the equilateral triangle, or the circle, the triangle and the square. The spaces which are left should be covered with the tablets of plain wood. Gradually the frame is completely filled with figures ; first, with very dissimilar figures, as, for example, a square, a very narrow rectangle, a triangle, a circle, an ellipse and a hexagon, or with other figures in combination.

Afterwards the teacher's object will be to arrange figures similar to one another in the frame, as, for example, the set of six rectangles, six triangles, six circles varying in size, etc.

This exercise resembles that of the cylinders. The insets are held by the buttons and taken from their places. They are then mixed on the table and the child is invited to put them back in their places. Here also the control of the error is in the *material*, for the figure cannot be inserted perfectly except when it is put in its own place. Hence a series of " experiments," of " attempts "

which end in victory.   The child is led to compare the various forms; to realise in a concrete
way the differences between them when an inset
wrongly placed will not go into the aperture.   In

FIG. 24.—CHILD TOUCHING THE INSETS.   (Montessori School,
Runton.)

this way he educates his eye to the *recognition
of forms.*

The new movement of the hand which the child
must co-ordinate is of particular importance.
He is taught to *touch the outline of the geometrical
figures* with the soft tips of the index and middle
finger of the right hand, or of the left as well, if
one believes in ambidexterity.   The child is made

to touch the outline, not only of the *inset* but also of the corresponding aperture, and only after *having touched* them is he to put back the inse into its place.

The *recognition* of the form is rendered much easier in this way. Children who evidently do not *recognise identities of form* by the eye and who make absurd attempts to place the most diverse figures one within the other, *do recognise* the forms after having touched their outlines, and arrange them very quickly in their right places.

The child's hand during this exercise of touching the outlines of the geometrical figures has a concrete guide in the object. This is especially true when he touches the frames, for his two fingers have only to follow the edge of the frame, which acts as an obstacle and is a very clear guide. The teacher must always intervene at the start to teach accurately this movement, which will have such an importance in the future. She must, therefore, show the child *how to touch*, not only by performing the movement herself slowly and clearly, but also by guiding the child's hand itself during his first attempts, so that he is sure to touch all the details—angles and sides. When his hand has learned to perform these movements with precision and accuracy, he will be *really* capable of following the outline of a geometrical figure, and through many repetitions of the exercise he will come to co-ordinate the movement necessary for the exact delineation of its form.

This exercise may be called an indirect but very real preparation for drawing. It is certainly the preparation of the hand to *trace an enclosed form*. The little hand which touches, feels, and knows how to follow a determined outline, is preparing itself, without knowing it, for writing.

The children make a special point of touching the outlines of the plane insets with accuracy. They themselves have invented the exercise of blindfolding their eyes so as to recognise the forms by touch only, taking out and putting back the insets without seeing them.

Corresponding to every form reproduced in the plane insets there are three white cards square in shape and of exactly the same size as the wooden frames of the insets. These cards are kept in three special cardboard boxes, almost cubic in form (Fig. 25).

On the cards are repeated, in three series, the

same geometrical forms as those of the plane
insets. The same measurements of the figures
also are exactly reproduced.

FIG. 25.—SERIES OF CARDS WITH GEOMETRICAL FORMS.

In the first series the forms are filled in, *i.e.*,
they are cut out in blue paper and gummed on
to the card ; in the second series there is only an

outline about half a centimetre in width, which is cut out in the same blue paper and gummed to the card ; in the third series, however, the geometrical figures are instead outlined only in black ink.

By the use of this second piece of the material, the exercise of the eye is gradually brought to perfection in the recognition of " plane forms." In fact, there is no longer the concrete control of error in the material as there was in the *wooden* insets, but the child, by his eye alone, must judge of identities of form when, instead of *fitting* the wooden forms into their corresponding apertures, he simply *rests* them on the cardboard figure.

Again, the refinement of the eye's power of discrimination increases every time the child passes from one series of cards to the next, and by the time that he has reached the third series, he can see the relation between a wooden object, which he holds in his hand, and an outline drawing ; that is, he can connect the concrete reality with an *abstraction*.   The *line* now assumes in his eyes a very definite meaning ; and he accustoms himself to recognise, to interpret and to judge of forms contained by a simple outline.

The exercises are various ; the children themselves invent them. Some love to spread out a number of the figures of the geometric insets before their eyes, and then, taking a handful of the cards and mixing them like playing cards, deal them out as quickly as possible, choosing the figures corresponding to the pieces. Then, as a test of their choice, they place the wooden pieces upon the forms on the cards. At this exercise they often cover whole tables, putting the wooden figures above, and beneath each one in a vertical line, the three corresponding forms of the cardboard series.

Another game invented by the children consists in putting out and mixing all the cards of the three series on two or three adjoining tables. The child then takes a wooden geometrical form and places it, as quickly as possible, on the corresponding cards which he has recognised at a glance among all the rest.

Four or five children play this game together, and as soon as one of them has found, for example, the filled-in figure corresponding to the wooden piece, and has placed the piece carefully and precisely upon it, another child takes away the piece in order to place it on the same form in outline. The game is somewhat suggestive of chess.

Many children, without any suggestion from

anyone, touch with the finger the outline of the figures in the three series of cards, doing it with seriousness of purpose, interest and perseverance.

We teach the children to name all the forms of the plane insets.

At first I had intended to limit my teaching to the most important names, such as square, rectangle, circle. But the children wanted to know all the names, taking pleasure in learning even the most difficult, such as trapezium, and decagon. They also show great pleasure in listening to the exact pronunciation of new words and in their repetition. Early childhood is, in fact, the age in which language is formed, and in which the sounds of a foreign language can be perfectly learnt.

When the child has had long practice with the plane insets, he begins to make " discoveries " in his environment, recognising forms, colours and qualities already known to him—a result which, in general, follows after all the sensory exercises. Then it is that a great enthusiasm is aroused in him, and the world becomes for him a source of pleasure. A little boy, walking one day alone on the roof terrace, repeated to himself with a thoughtful expression on his face, " The sky is blue ! the sky is blue ! "   Once a cardinal, an admirer of the children of the school in Via Guisti, wished himself to bring them some biscuits and to enjoy the sight of a little greediness among the children.   When he had finished his distribution, instead of seeing the children put the food hastily into their mouths, to his great surprise he heard them call out, " A triangle ! a circle ! a rectangle ! "   In fact, these biscuits were made in geometrical shapes.

In one of the people's dwellings at Milan, a mother, preparing the dinner in the kitchen, took from a packet a slice of bread and butter.   Her little four-year-old boy who was with her said, " Rectangle."   The woman going on with her work cut off a large corner of the slice of bread, and the child cried out, " Triangle."   She put this bit into the saucepan, and the child, looking at the piece that was left, called out more loudly than before, " And now it is a trapezium."

The father, a working man, who was present, was much impressed with the incident.   He went straight to look for the teacher and asked for an explanation.   Much moved, he said, " If I had been educated in that way I should not be now just an ordinary workman."

It was he who later on arranged for a demonstration to induce all the workmen of the dwellings to take an interest in the school. They ended by presenting the teacher with a parchment they had painted themselves, and on it, between the pictures of little children, they had introduced every kind of geometrical form.

As regards the touching of objects for the realisation of their form, there is an infinite field of discovery open to the child in his environment. Children have been seen to stand opposite a beautiful pillar or a statue and, after having admired it, to close their eyes in a state of beatitude and pass their hands many times over the forms. One of our teachers met one day in a church two little brothers from the school in Via Guisti. They were standing looking at the small columns supporting the altar. Little by little the elder boy edged nearer the columns and began to touch them, then, as if he desired his little brother to share his pleasure, he drew him nearer and, taking his hand very gently, made him pass it round the smooth and beautiful shape of the column. But a sacristan came up at that moment and sent away " those tiresome children who were touching everything."

The great pleasure which the children derive from the recognition of objects by touching their form corresponds in itself to a sensory exercise. Many psychologists have spoken of the *stereognostic* sense, that is, the capacity of recognising forms by the movement of the muscles of the hand as it follows the outlines of solid objects. This sense does not consist only of the sense of touch, because the tactile sensation is only that by which we perceive the differences in quality of surfaces (rough or smooth). Perception of form comes from the combination of two sensations, tactile and muscular, muscular sensations being sensations of movement. What we call in the blind the *tactile* sense is in reality more often the stereognostic sense. That is, they perceive by means of their hands the *form of bodies*.

It is the special muscular sensibility of the child from three to six years of age, who is forming *his own muscular activity*, which stimulates him to use the stereognostic sense. When the child spontaneously blindfolds his eyes in order to recognise various objects, such as the plane and solid insets, he is exercising this sense.

There are many exercises which he can do to enable him to recognise with closed eyes objects of well-defined shapes, as, for example, the little bricks and cubes of Froebel, marbles, coins, beans, peas, etc. From a selection of different objects mixed together he can pick out those that are alike, and arrange them in separate heaps.

In the didactic material there are also geometrical solids—pale blue in colour—a sphere, a prism, a pyramid, a cone, a cylinder. The most attractive way of teaching a child to recognise these forms is for him to touch them with closed eyes and to guess their names, the latter being learnt in a way which I will describe later. After an exercise of this kind the child observes the forms when his eyes are open with a much more lively interest. Another way of interesting him in the solid geometrical forms is to make them *move*. The sphere rolls in every direction; the cylinder rolls in one direction only; the cone rolls round itself; the prism and the pyramid, however, stand still, but the prism falls over more easily than the pyramid.

Little more remains of the didactic material for the education of the senses. There is, however, a series of six cardboard cylinders, either closed entirely or with wooden covers (Fig. 26).

When these cases are shaken they produce sounds varying in intensity from loud to almost imperceptible sounds, according to the nature of the objects inside the cylinder.

There is a double set of these, and the exercise

FIG. 26.—SOUND BOXES.

consists, first, in the recognition of sounds of equal intensity, arranging the cylinders in pairs. The next exercise consists in the comparison of one sound with another; that is, the child arranges the six cylinders in a series according to the loudness of the sound which they produce. The exercise is analogous to that with the colour spools, which also are paired and then arranged

in gradation. In this case also the child performs the exercise seated comfortably at a table.
After a preliminary explanation from the teacher
he repeats the exercise by himself, his eyes being
blindfolded that he may better concentrate his
attention.

We may conclude with a general rule for the
direction of the education of the senses.   The order
of procedure should be :

(1) Recognition of *identities* (the pairing of
similar objects and the insertion of solid forms into
places which fit them).

(2) Recognition of *contrasts* (the presentation
of the extremes of a series of objects).

(3) Discrimination between objects very *similar*
to one another.

To concentrate the attention of the child upon
the sensory stimulus which is acting upon him at
a particular moment, it is well, as far as possible,
to *isolate* the sense; for instance, to obtain silence
in the room for all the exercises and to blindfold
the eyes for those particular exercises which do
not relate to the education of the sense of sight.

The cinematograph pictures give a general idea
of all the sense exercises which the children
can do with the material, and anyone who has

been initiated into the theory on which these are based will be able gradually to recognise them as they are seen practically carried out.

It is very advisable for those who wish to guide the children in these sensory exercises to begin themselves by working with the didactic material. The experience will give them some idea of what the children must feel, of the difficulties which they must overcome, etc., and, up to a certain point, it will give them some conception of the interest which these exercises can arouse in them. Whoever makes such experiments himself will be most struck by the fact that, when blindfolded, he finds that all the sensations of touch and hearing really appear more acute and are more easily recognised. On account of this alone no small interest will be aroused in the experimenter.

For the beginning of the education of the musical sense, we use in Rome a material which does not form part of the didactic apparatus as it is sold at present. It consists of a double series of bells forming an octave with tones and semitones. These metal bells, which stand upon a wooden rectangular base, are all alike in appearance, but, when struck with a little wooden hammer, give out sounds corresponding to the notes doh, re, mi, fah, soh, lah, te, doh, doh ♯, re ♯, fah ♯, soh ♯, lah ♯.

One series of bells is arranged in chromatic order upon a long board, upon which are painted rectangular spaces which are black and white and of the same size as the bases which support the bells. As on a pianoforte keyboard, the white spaces correspond to the tones, and the black to the semitones (Fig. 27).

At first the only bells to be arranged upon the board are those which correspond to the tones ; these are set upon the white spaces in the order of the musical notes doh, re, mi, fah, soh, lah, te, doh.

To perform the first exercise the child strikes with a small hammer the first note of the series already arranged, *doh*. Then among a second series of corresponding bells which, arranged without the semitones. are mixed together upon the table, he tries, by striking them one after the other, to find the sound which is the same as

FIG. 27.—MUSICAL BELLS.

the first one he has struck (doh). When he has succeeded in finding the corresponding sound, he puts the bell thus chosen opposite the first one (doh) upon the board. Then he strikes the second bell, *re,* once or twice ; then from among the mixed group of bells he makes experiments until he recognises *re,* which he places opposite the second bell of the series already arranged. He continues in the same way right to the end, looking for the identity of the sounds and performing an exercise of " *pairing* " similar to that already done in the case of the sound boxes, the colours, etc.

Later, he learns in order the sounds of the musical scale, striking in rapid succession the bells arranged in order, and also accompanying his action with his voice—doh, re, mi, fah, soh, lah, te, doh. When he is able to recognise and *remember* the series of sounds, the child takes the eight bells and, after mixing them up, he tries, by striking them with the hammer, to find " *doh,*" then " *re,*" etc. Every time that he takes a new note, he strikes from the beginning all the bells already recognised and arranged in order—doh, *re ;* doh, re, *mi ;* doh, re, mi, *fah ;* doh, re, mi, fah, *soh,* etc. In this way he succeeds in arranging all the bells in the order of the scale, guided only by his ear, and having succeeded, he strikes all the notes one after the other up and down the scale. This exercise fascinates children from five years old upwards.

If the objects which have been described constitute the didactic material for the beginnings of a methodical education of the auditory sense, I have no desire to limit to them an educational process which is so important and already so complex in its practice, whether in the long established methods of treatment for the deaf, or in modern physiological musical education. In fact, I also use resonant metal tubes, small bars of wood which emit musical notes, and strings (little harps), upon which the children seek to recognise the tones they have already learnt with the exercise of the bells. The pianoforte may also be used for the same purpose. In this way the difference in *timbre* comes to be perceived together with the differences in tone. At the same time various exercises, already mentioned, such as the marches played on the piano for rhythmic exercises, and the simple songs sung by the children themselves, offer extensive means for the development of the musical sense.

To quicken the child's attention in special relation to sounds there is a most important exercise which, contrary to all attempts made up to this time in the practice of education, consists not in producing but in eliminating, as far as possible, all sounds from the environment. My " lesson of silence " has been very widely applied, even in schools where the rest of my method has not found its way, for the sake of its practical effect upon the discipline of the children.

The children are taught " not to move " ; to inhibit all those motor impulses which may arise from any cause whatsoever, and in order to induce in them real " immobility," it is necessary to initiate them in the *control* of all their movements. The teacher, then, does not limit herself to saying, " Sit still," but she gives them the example herself, showing them how to sit absolutely still, that is, with feet still, body still, arms still, head still. The respiratory movements should also be performed in such a way as to produce no sound.

The children must be taught how to succeed in this exercise. The fundamental condition is that of finding a comfortable position, *i.e.*, a position of equilibrium. As they are seated for this exercise, they must therefore make themselves comfortable either in their little chairs or on the ground. When immobility is obtained, the room is half-darkened, or else the children close their eyes, or cover them with their hands.

It is quite plain to see that the children take a great interest in the " Silence " ; they seem to give themselves up to a kind of spell, they might be said to be wrapped in meditation. Little by little, as each child, watching himself, becomes more and more still, the silence deepens till it becomes absolute and can be felt, just as the twilight gradually deepens whilst the sun is setting.

Then it is that slight sounds, unnoticed before, are heard ; the ticking of the clock, the chirp of a sparrow in the garden, the flight of a butterfly. The world becomes full of imperceptible sounds which invade that deep silence without disturbing it, just as the stars shine out in the dark sky without banishing the darkness of the night.

It is almost the discovery of a new world, where there is rest. It is, as it were, the twilight of the world of loud noises and of the uproar that oppresses the spirit. At such a time the spirit is set free, and opens out like the corolla of the convolvulus.

And leaving metaphor for the reality of facts, can we not all recall feelings that have possessed us at sunset, when all the vivid impressions of the day, the brightness and clamour, are silenced? It is not that we miss the day, but that our spirit expands. It becomes more sensitive to the inner play of emotions, strong and persistent, or changeful and serene.

> " It was that hour when mariners feel longing,
> And hearts grow tender."
>
> (Dante, Trans. Longfellow.)

The lesson of silence ends with a general calling of the children's names. The teacher, or one of the children, takes her place behind the class or in an adjoining room, and " calls " the motionless children, one by one, by name; the call is made in a whisper, that is, without vocal sound. This demands a close attention on the part of the child, if he is to hear his name. When his name is called he must rise and find his way to the voice which called him; his movements must be light and vigilant, and so well controlled *as to make no noise.*

When the children have become acquainted with *silence,* their hearing is in a manner refined for the perception of sounds. Those sounds which are too loud become gradually displeasing to the

ear of one who has known the pleasure of silence,
and has discovered the world of delicate sounds.
From this point the children gradually go on to
perfect themselves ; they walk lightly, take care
not to knock against the furniture, move their
chairs without noise, and place things upon the
table with great care. The result of this is seen
in the grace of carriage and of movement, which
is especially delightful on account of the way in
which it has been brought about. It is not a
grace taught externally for the sake of beauty
or regard for the world, but one which is born of
the pleasure felt by the spirit in immobility and
silence. The soul of the child wishes to free itself
from the irksomeness of sounds that are too loud,
from obstacles to its peace during work. These
children, with the grace of pages to a noble lord,
are serving their spirits.

This exercise develops very definitely the social
spirit. No other lesson, no other " situation,"
could do the same. A profound silence can be
obtained even when more than fifty children are
crowded together in a small space, provided that
all the children know how to keep still and want
to do it ; but one disturber is enough to take
away the charm.

Here is a demonstration of the co-operation of all the members of a community to achieve a common end. The children gradually show increased power of *inhibition;* many of them, rather than disturb the silence, refrain from brushing a fly off the nose or suppress a cough or sneeze. The same exhibition of collective action is seen in the care with which the children move to avoid making a noise during their work. The lightness with which they run on tiptoe, the grace with which they shut a cupboard, or lay an object on the table, these are qualities that must be *acquired by all*, if the environment is to become tranquil and free from disturbance. One rebel is sufficient to mar this achievement; one noisy child, walking on his heels or banging the door, can disturb the peaceful atmosphere of the small community.

LANGUAGE AND KNOWLEDGE OF THE WORLD

The special importance of the sense of hearing comes from the fact that it is the sense connected with speech. Therefore, to train the child's attention to follow sounds and noises which are produced in the environment, to recognise them and to discriminate between them, is to prepare his attention to follow more accurately the sounds of articulate language. The teacher must be careful to pronounce clearly and completely the sounds of the word when she speaks to a child, even though she may be speaking in a low voice, almost as if telling him a secret. The children's songs are also a good means for obtaining exact pronunciation. The teacher, when she teaches them, pronounces slowly, separating the component sounds of the word pronounced.

But a special opportunity for training in clear and exact speech occurs when the lessons are given in the nomenclature relating to the sensory exercises. In every exercise, when the child has *recognised* the differences between the qualities of the objects, the teacher fixes the idea of this quality with a word. Thus, when the child has many times built and rebuilt the tower of the pink cubes, at an opportune moment the teacher draws near him, and taking the two extreme cubes, the largest and the smallest, and showing them to him, says, " This is large "; " this is small." The two words only, " large " and " small," are pronounced several times in succession with strong emphasis and with a very clear pronunciation, " This is *large*, large, large ";

after which there is a moment's pause. Then the teacher, to see if the child has understood, verifies with the following tests : " Give me the large one. Give me the *small* one." Again, " the . . . *large* one." " Now the small one." " Give me the large one." Then there is another pause. Finally, the teacher, pointing to the objects in turn asks, " What is this ? " The child, if he has learned, replies rightly, " Large," " Small." The teacher then urges the child to repeat the words always more clearly and as accurately as possible. " What is it ? " " Large." " What ? " " Large." " Tell me nicely, what is it ? " " Large."

_ *Large* and *small* objects are those which differ only in size and not in form, that is, all three dimensions change more or less proportionally. We should say that a house is " large " and a hut is " small." When two pictures represent the same objects in different dimensions one can be said to be an enlargement of the other.

When, however, only the dimensions referring to the section of the object change, whilst the length remains the same, the objects are respectively " thick " and " thin." We should say of two posts of equal height, but different cross-

section, that one is " thick " and the other is
" thin." The teacher, therefore, gives a lesson
on the brown prisms similar to that with the cubes
in the three " periods " which I have described:

Period 1. *Naming.* "This is thick. This is
thin."

Period 2. *Recognition.* " Give me the *thick.*
Give me the *thin.*"

Period 3. *The Pronunciation of the Word.*
" What is this ? "

There is a way of helping the child to recognise
differences in dimension and to place the objects
in correct gradation. After the lesson which I
have described, the teacher scatters the brown
prisms, for instance, on a carpet, says to the
child, " Give me the thickest of all," and lays the
object on a table. Then, again, she invites the
child to look for *the thickest* piece among those
scattered on the floor, and every time the piece
chosen is laid in its order on the table next to
the piece previously chosen. In this way the
child accustoms himself always to look either
for the *thickest* or the *thinnest* among the rest, and
so has a guide to help him to lay the pieces in
gradation.

When there is one dimension only which varies,

as in the case of the rods, the objects are said to
be " long " and " short," the varying dimension
being length. When the varying dimension is
height, the objects are said to be " tall " and
" short " ; when the breadth varies, they are
" broad " and " narrow."

Of these three varieties we offer the child as
a fundamental lesson only that in which the
length varies, and we teach the differences by
means of the usual " three periods," and by ask-
ing him to select from the pile at one time
always the " longest," at another always the
" shortest."

The child in this way acquires great accuracy
in the use of words. One day the teacher had
ruled the blackboard with very fine lines. A
child said, " What small lines ! " " They are
not small," corrected another ; " they are *thin*."

When the names to be taught are those of
colours or of forms, so that it is not necessary to
emphasise contrast between extremes, the teacher
can give more than two names at the same time,
as, for instance, " This is red." " This is blue."
" This is yellow." Or, again, " This is a square."
" This is a triangle." " This is a circle." In
the case of a *gradation*, however, the teacher will

select (if she is teaching the colours) the two extremes " dark " and " light," then making choice always of the " darkest " and the " lightest."

Many of the lessons here described can be seen in the cinematograph pictures; lessons on touching the plane insets and the surfaces, in walking on the line, in colour memory, in the nomenclature relating to the cubes and the long rods, in the composition of words, reading, writing, etc.

By means of these lessons the child comes to know many words very thoroughly—large, small ; thick, thin ; long, short ; dark, light ; rough, smooth ; heavy, light ; hot, cold, tepid ; and the names of many colours and geometrical forms. Such words do not relate to any particular *object*, but to a psychic acquisition on the part of the child. In fact, the name is given *after a long exercise*, in which the child, concentrating his attention on different qualities of objects, has made comparisons, reasoned, and formed judgments, until he has acquired a power of discrimination which he did not possess before. In a word, he has *refined his senses ;* his observation of things has been thorough and fundamental; he has *changed himself*.

He finds himself, therefore, facing the world with *psychic* qualities refined and quickened. His powers of observation and of recognition have greatly increased. Further, the mental images which he has succeeded in establishing are not a confused medley ; they are all classified—forms are distinct from dimensions, and dimensions are classed according to the qualities which result from the combinations of varying dimensions. All these are quite distinct from *gradations*. Colours are divided according to tint and to depth of tone, silence is distinct from non-silence, noises from sounds, and everything has its own exact and appropriate name. The child then has not only developed in himself special qualities of observation and of judgment, but the objects which he observes, one may say, go of their own accord into their place, according to the order established in his mind, and they are placed under their appropriate name in an exact classification.

Does not the student of the experimental sciences prepare himself in a similar way to observe the outside world ? He may find himself, like the uneducated man, in the midst of the most diverse natural objects, but he differs from the latter in that he has *special qualities* for observation. If he is a worker with the microscope, his eyes are accustomed to see in the field of the micro-scope particulars which the ordinary man cannot distinguish. If he is an astronomer, he will look through the same telescope as the curious visitor or *dilettante*, but he will see much more clearly. The same plants surround the botanist and the ordinary wayfarer, but the botanist sees in every plant those qualities which are classified in his mind, and assigns to each plant its own place in the natural orders, giving it its exact name. It is this capacity for recognising a plant in a complex order of classification which distinguishes the botanist from the ordinary gardener, and it is *exact* and scientific language which characterises the trained observer.

Now, the scientist who has developed special qualities of observation and who " possesses " an order in which to classify external objects will be the man to make scientific *discoveries*. It will never be he who, without preparation and order, wanders dreaming among the plants or beneath the star-lit sky.

This is the difference between our children and those who are left to receive their external impressions, as it were, in chaos.

In fact, our little ones have the impression of continually "making discoveries" in the world about them: and in this they find the greatest joy. They take from the world a knowledge which is ordered and which inspires them with enthusiasm. Into their minds there enters "the Creation" instead of "the Chaos;" and it seems that their souls find therein a divine exultation.

FREEDOM

The success of these results is closely connected with the delicate intervention of the one who guides the children in their development. It is necessary for the teacher to *guide* the child without letting him feel her presence too much, so that she may be always ready to supply the desired help, but may never be the obstacle between the child and his experience.

A *lesson* in the ordinary use of the word cools the child's enthusiasm for the *knowledge of things*, just as it would cool the enthusiasm of adults. To keep alive that enthusiasm is the secret of real guidance, and it will not prove a difficult task, provided that the attitude towards the child's acts be that of respect, calm and waiting, and provided that he be left free in his movements and in his experiences.

Then we shall notice that the child has a personality which is seeking to expand; he has initiative, he chooses his own work, persists in it, changes it according to his inner needs; he does not shirk effort, he rather goes in search of it and with great joy overcomes obstacles within his capacity. He is sociable to the extent of wanting to share with everyone his successes, his discoveries, and his little triumphs. There is therefore no need of intervention. "Wait while observing." That is the motto for the educator.

Let us wait, and be always ready to share in both the joys and the difficulties which the child experiences. He himself invites our sympathy, and we should respond fully and gladly. Let us have endless patience with his slow progress, and show enthusiasm and gladness at his successes. If we could say: "We are respectful and courteous in our dealings with children, we treat them as we should like to be treated ourselves," we should certainly have mastered a great educational principle and undoubtedly be setting an *example of good education*.

What we all desire for ourselves, namely, not to

friends

be disturbed in our work, not to find hindrances to our efforts, to have good friends ready to help us in times of need, to see them rejoice with us, to be on terms of equality with them, to be able to confide and trust in them—this is what we need for happy companionship. In the same way children are human beings to whom respect is due, superior to us by virtue of their innocence and of the greater possibilities of their future. What we desire they desire also.

As a rule, however, we do not respect our children. We try to force them to follow us without regard to their special needs. We are overbearing with them, and above all, rude; and then we expect them to be submissive and well-behaved, knowing all the time how strong is their instinct of imitation and how touching their faith in and admiration of us. They will imitate us in any case. Let us treat them, therefore, with all the kindness which we would wish to develop in them.

And by kindness is not meant caresses. Should we not call anyone who embraced us at the first time of meeting rude, vulgar and ill-bred ? Kindness consists in interpreting the wishes of others, in conforming one's self to them, and sacrificing, if need be, one's own desire. This is the kindness which we must show towards children.

To find the interpretation of children's desires we must study them scientifically, for their desires are often unconscious. They are the inner cry of life, which wishes to unfold according to mysterious laws. We know very little of the way in which it unfolds. Certainly the child is growing into a man by force of a divine action similar to that by which from nothing he became a child.

Our intervention in this marvellous process is *indirect;* we are here to offer to this life, which came into the world by itself, the *means* necessary for its development, and having done that, we must await this development with respect.

Let us leave the life *free* to develop within the limits of the good, and let us observe this inner life developing. This is the whole of our mission. Perhaps, as we watch, we shall be reminded of the words of Him who was absolutely good, "Suffer the little children to come unto Me." That is to say, " Do not hinder them from coming, since, if they are left free and unhampered, they will come."

WRITING

The child who has completed all the exercises above described, and is thus *prepared* for an advance towards unexpected conquests, is about four years old.

He is not an unknown quantity, as are children who have been left to gain varied and casual experiences by themselves, and who therefore differ in type and intellectual standard, not only according to their "natures," but especially according to the chances and opportunities they have found for their spontaneous inner formation.

Education has *determined* for our children *an environment.* Individual differences to be found in them can, therefore, be put down almost exclusively to each one's individual "nature." Owing to their environment, which offers *means* adapted and measured to meet the needs of their psychical development, our children have acquired a fundamental type which is common to all. They have *co-ordinated* their movements in various kinds of manual work about the house, and so have acquired a characteristic independence of action, and an initiative in the adaptation of their actions to their environment, and out of all this there emerges a *personality*, for the children have become little men, who are self-reliant.

The special attention necessary to handle small fragile objects without breaking them, and to move heavy articles without making a noise, has endowed the movements of the whole body with a lightness and grace which are characteristic of our children. It is a deep feeling of "responsibility" which has brought them to such a pitch of perfection. For instance, when they carry three or four tumblers at a time, or a tureen of hot soup, they know that they are responsible not only for the objects, but also for the success of the meal which at that moment they are directing. In the same way each child feels the responsibility of the "silence," of the prevention of harsh sounds, and he knows how to co-operate for the general good in keeping the environment, not only orderly, but quiet and calm. Indeed, our children have taken the road which leads them to mastery of themselves.

But their formation is due to a deeper psychological work still, arising from the education of the senses. In addition to ordering their environment and ordering themselves in their outward personalities, they have also ordered the inner world of their minds.

The didactic material, in fact, does not offer to the child the "content" of the mind, but the *order* for that "content." It causes him to distinguish identities from differences, extreme differences from fine gradations, and to classify, under conceptions of quality and of quantity, the most varying sensations appertaining to surfaces, colours, dimensions, forms and sounds. The mind has formed itself by a special exercise of attention, observing, comparing, and classifying.

The mental attitude acquired by such an exercise leads the child to make ordered observations of the environment, observations which prove as interesting to him as discoveries, and so stimulate him to multiply them indefinitely and to form in his mind a rich "content" of clear ideas.

Language now comes to *fix* by means of *exact words* the ideas which the mind has acquired. These words are few in number and have reference, not to separate objects, but rather to the *order of the ideas* which have been formed in the mind. In this way the children are able to "find themselves," alike in the world of natural things and in the world of words which surrounds them, for they have an inner guide which leads them to become *active and intelligent explorers* instead of wandering wayfarers in an unknown land.

These are the children who, in a short space of time, sometimes in a few days, learn to write and to perform the first operations in arithmetic. It is not a fact that children in general can do it, as many have believed. It is not a case of giving my material for writing to unprepared children and of awaiting the " miracle."

The fact is that the minds and hands of our children are already *prepared* for writing, and ideas of quantity, identity, difference, and gradation, which form the basis of all calculation, have been maturing for a long time in them. One might say, indeed, that all their previous education is a preparation for the first stages of essential culture—*writing, reading, and number*, and that knowledge comes as an easy, spontaneous, and logical consequence of the preparation, that it is in fact its natural *conclusion*.

We have already seen that the purpose of the *word* is to fix ideas and to facilitate the elementary comprehension of *things*. In the same way writing and arithmetic now fix the complex inner acquisitions of the mind, which proceeds henceforward continually to enrich itself by fresh observations.

Our children have long been preparing the hand for writing. Throughout all the sensory exercises, the hand, whilst co-operating with the mind in its attainments and in its work of formation, was preparing its own future. When the hand learnt to hold itself lightly suspended over a horizontal surface in order to touch rough and smooth, when it took the cylinders of the solid insets and placed them in their apertures, when with two fingers it touched the outlines of the geometrical forms, it was co-ordinating movements, and the child is now ready—almost impatient to use them in the fascinating "synthesis" of writing.

The *direct* preparation for writing also consists in exercises of the movements of the hand. There are two series of exercises, quite different from one another. I have analysed the movements which are connected with writing, and prepare them separately one from the other. When we write, we perform a movement for the *management* of the instrument of writing, a movement which generally acquires an individual character, so that a person's handwriting can be recognised, and, in certain medical cases, changes in the nervous system can be traced by the corresponding alterations in the handwriting. In fact, it is from the handwriting that specialists in that subject would interpret the *moral character* of individuals.

Writing has, besides this, a general character, which has reference to the form of the alphabetical signs.

When a man writes he combines these two parts, but they actually exist as the *component parts of a single product* and can be prepared apart.

Exercises for the Management of the Instrument of Writing

(The Individual Part.)

In the didactic material there are two sloping wooden boards, on each of which stand four square metal frames, coloured pink. In each of these is inserted a blue geometrical figure similar to the geometric insets and provided with a small button for a handle. With this material we use a box of ten coloured pencils and a little album of designs which I have prepared after five years' experience of observing the children. I have chosen and graduated the designs according to the use which the children made of them.

The two sloping boards are set side by side in line, and on them are placed eight complete " insets," that is to say, frames with geometrical figures. The child is given a sheet of white paper and the box of ten coloured pencils. He will then

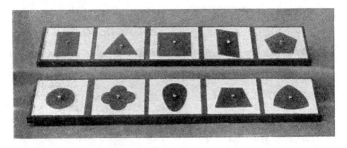

FIG. 28.—SLOPING BOARDS TO DISPLAY SET OF METAL INSETS.

choose one of the eight metal insets, which are arranged in an attractive line at a certain distance from him. The child is taught the following process :

He lays the frame of the metal inset on the sheet of paper, and, holding it down firmly with one hand, he follows with a coloured pencil the interior outline which describes a geometrical figure. Then he lifts the square frame, and finds drawn

upon the paper an enclosed geometrical form, a
triangle, a circle, a hexagon, etc.   The child has
not actually performed a new exercise, because he
had already performed all these movements when
he *touched* the wooden plane insets.   The only
new feature of the exercise is that he follows the
outlines no longer directly with his finger, but
through the medium of a pencil.   That is, he
draws—he leaves a trace of his movement.

The child finds this exercise easy and most
interesting, and, as soon as he has succeeded in
making the first outline, he places above it the
piece of blue metal corresponding to it.   This is an
exercise exactly similar to that which he performed
when he placed the wooden geometrical figures
upon the cards of the third series, where the
figures are only contained by a simple line.

This time, however, when the action of placing
the form upon the outline is performed, the child
takes *another coloured pencil* and draws the outline
of the blue metal figure.

When he raises it, if the drawing is well done,
he finds upon the paper a geometrical figure
contained by two outlines in colours; if the
colours have been well chosen, the result is very
attractive, and the child, who has already had a

considerable education of the chromatic sense, is keenly interested in it.

These may seem unnecessary details, but, as a matter of fact, they are all important. For instance, if, instead of arranging the eight metal insets in a row, the teacher distributes them among the children without thus exhibiting them, the child's exercises are much limited. When, on the other hand, the insets are exhibited before his eyes, he feels the desire to draw them *all*, one after the other, and the number of exercises is multiplied.

The two *coloured outlines* rouse the desire of the child to see another combination of colours and then to repeat the experience. The variety of the objects and the colours are therefore an *inducement* to work and hence to the final success.

Here the actual preparatory movement for writing begins. When the child has drawn the figure in double outline, he takes hold of a pencil " like a pen for writing," and draws marks up and down until he has completely filled the figure. In this way a definite filled-in figure remains on the paper, similar to the figures on the cards of the first series. This figure can be in any of the ten colours. At first the children fill in the figures very clumsily without regard for the outlines, making very heavy lines and not keeping them parallel. Little by little, however, the drawings improve, in that they keep within the outlines, and the lines increase in number, grow finer, and are parallel to one another.

When the child has begun these exercises, he is filled with a desire to continue them, and never tires of drawing the outlines of the figures and then filling them in. Each child suddenly becomes the possessor of a considerable number of drawings, and he treasures them up in his own little drawer. In this way he *organises* the movement of writing, which brings him *to the management of the pen.* This movement in ordinary methods is represented by the wearisome pothook connected with the first laborious and tedious attempts at writing.

The organisation of this movement, which began with the guidance of a piece of metal, is as yet rough and imperfect, and the child now passes on to the *filling in of the prepared designs* in the little album. The leaves are taken from the book one by one in the order of progression in which they are arranged, and the child fills in the prepared designs with coloured pencils in the same way as before. Here the choice of the colours is another intelligent occupation which encourages the child to multiply the tasks. He chooses the colours by himself and with much taste. The delicacy of the shades which he chooses and the harmony with which he arranges them in these designs show us that the common belief, that children love *bright and glaring* colours, has been the result of observation of *children without education* who have been abandoned to the rough and harsh experiences of an environment unfitted for them.

The education of the chromatic sense becomes then, at this point of the child's development, the *lever* which enables him to become possessed of a firm, bold, and beautiful handwriting.

The drawings lend themselves to *limiting*, in the most varied ways, *the length of the strokes with which they are filled in.* The child will have to fill in geometrical figures, both large and small, of a pavement design, or flowers and leaves, or the various details of an animal or a landscape. In this way the hand accustoms itself, not only to perform the general action, but also to confine the movement within all kinds of limits.

Hence the child is preparing himself to write in a handwriting *either* large or small. Indeed, later on he will write as well between wide lines on a blackboard as between the narrow, closely-ruled lines of an exercise book generally used by much older children.

The number of exercises which the child performs with the drawings is practically un-limited. He will often take another coloured pencil and draw over again the outlines of the figure already filled in with colour. A help to the *continuation* of the exercise is to be found in the further education of the chromatic sense, which the child acquires by painting the same designs in water-colours. Later he mixes colours for himself until he can imitate the colours of nature, or create the delicate tints which his own imagina-tion desires. It is not possible, however, to speak of all this in detail within the limits of this small work.

Exercises for the Writing of Alphabetical Signs

In the didactic material there are series of boxes which contain the alphabetical signs. At this point we take those cards which are covered with very smooth paper, to which is gummed a letter of the alphabet cut out in sandpaper. There are also large cards on which are gummed several letters, grouped together according to analogy of form (Fig. 30).

The children " have to *touch* over the alphabetical signs, as though they were writing." They touch them with the tips of the index and middle fingers in the same way as when they touched the wooden insets, and with the hand raised, as when they lightly touched the rough and smooth surfaces.   The teacher herself touches the letters to show the child how

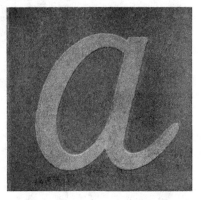

Fig.   29. — Single   Sandpaper Letter.

the movement should be performed, and the child, if he has had much practice in touching the wooden insets, *imitates* her with *ease* and pleasure. Without the previous practice, however, the child's hand does not follow the letter with accuracy, and it is most interesting to make close observations of the children in order to understand the importance of a *remote motor preparation* for writing, and also

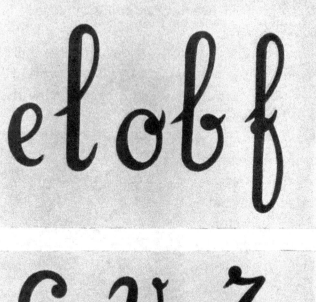

FIG. 30.—GROUPS OF SANDPAPER LETTERS.

to realise the *immense* strain which we impose upon children when we set them to write directly without a previous motor education of the hand.

The child finds great pleasure in touching the sandpaper letters. It is an exercise by which he applies to a new attainment the power he has already acquired through exercising the sense of touch. Whilst the child touches a letter, the teacher pronounces its sound, and she uses for the lesson the usual three periods. Thus, for example, presenting the two vowels, *i, o,* she will have the child touch them slowly and accurately, and repeat their relative sounds one after the other as the child touches them, i, i, i ! o, o, o ! Then she will say to the child : " Give me i ! " " Give me o ! " Finally, comes the question : " What is this ? " To which the child replies, " i," " o." She proceeds in the same way through all the other letters, giving, in the case of the consonants, not the name, but only the sound. The child then touches the letters by himself over and over again, either on the separate cards or on the large cards on which several letters are gummed, and in this way he establishes the movements necessary for tracing the alphabetical signs. At the same time he retains the *visual* image of the letter. This process forms the first preparation, not only for writing, but also for reading, because it is evident that when the child *touches* the letters he performs the movement corresponding to the writing of them, and, at the same time, when he recognises them by sight he is reading the alphabet.

The child has thus prepared, in effect, all the necessary movements for writing; therefore he *can write*. This important conquest is the result of a long period of inner formation of which the child is not clearly aware. But a day will come —very soon—when he *will write*, and that will be a day of great surprise for him—the wonderful harvest of an unknown sowing.

The alphabet of movable letters cut out in pink and blue cardboard, and kept in a special box with compartments, serves " for the composition of words " (Fig. 31).

In a phonetic language, like Italian, it is enough to pronounce clearly the different component sounds of a word (as, for example, m-a-n-o), so that the child whose ear is *already educated* may recognise one by one the component sounds. Then he looks in the movable alphabet for the *signs* corresponding to each sound, and lays them one beside the other, thus composing the word (for instance, mano). Gradually he will

FIG. 31.—BOX OF MOVABLE LETTERS.

become able to do the same thing with words of which he thinks himself ; he succeeds in breaking them up into their component sounds, and in translating them into a row of signs.

When the child has composed the words in this

way, he knows how to read them.   In this method, therefore, all the processes leading to writing include reading as well.

If the language is not phonetic, the teacher can compose separate words with the movable alphabet and then pronounce them, letting the child repeat by himself the exercise of arranging and re-reading them.

In the material there are two movable alphabets. One of them consists of larger letters, and is divided into two boxes, each of which contains the vowels.   This is used for the first exercises, in which the child needs very large objects in order to recognise the letters.   When he is acquainted with one half of the consonants he can begin to compose words, even though he is dealing with one part only of the alphabet.

The other movable alphabet has smaller letters and is contained in a single box.   It is given to children who have made their first attempts at composition with words, and already know the complete alphabet.

It is after these exercises with the movable alphabet that the child *is able to write entire words*.   This phenomenon generally occurs unexpectedly, and then a child who has never yet traced a stroke or a letter on paper *writes several words in succession*. From that moment he continues to write, always gradually perfecting himself.

This spontaneous writing takes on the characteristics of a *natural* phenomenon, and the child who has begun to write the " first word " will continue to write, just as he spoke after pronouncing the first word, and as he walked after having taken the first step. The same course of inner formation through which the phenomenon of writing appeared is the course of his future progress, of his growth to perfection.

The child prepared in this way has entered upon a course of development through which he will pass as surely as the growth of the body and the development of the natural functions pass through their course of development when life has once been established.

For the interesting and very complex phenomena relating to the development of writing and then of reading see my larger works.

THE READING OF MUSIC

When the child knows how to read, he can make a first application of this knowledge to the reading of the names of musical notes.

In connection with the material for sensory education, consisting of the series of bells, we use a didactic material, which serves as an introduction to musical reading. For this purpose we have, in the first place, a wooden board, not very long, and painted pale green. On this board the staff is cut out in black, and in every line and space are cut round holes, inside each of which is written the name of the note in its reference to the treble clef.

There is also a series of little white discs which can be fitted into the holes. On one side of each disc is written the name of the note (doh, re, mi, fah, soh, lah, te, doh).

The child, guided by the name written on the discs, puts them, with the name uppermost, in their right places on the board and then reads the names of the notes. This exercise he can do by himself, and he learns the position of each note on the staff. Another exercise which the child can do at the same time is to place the disc bearing the name of the note on the rectangular base of the corresponding bell, whose sound he has already learned to recognise by ear in the sensorial exercise described above.

Following this exercise there is another staff

made on a board of green wood, which is longer than the other and has neither indentures nor signs. A considerable number of discs, on one side of which are written the names of the notes, is at the disposal of the child. He takes up a disc at random, reads its name and places it on the staff, with the name underneath, so that the white face

FIG. 32.—THE MUSICAL STAFF.*

of the disc shows on the top. By the repetition of this exercise the child is enabled to arrange many discs on the same line or in the same space. When he has finished, he turns them all over so that the names are outside, and so finds out if he has made mistakes. After learning the treble clef the child passes on to learn the bass with great ease.

* The single staff is used in the Conservatoire of Milan and utilized in the Perlasca method.

To the staff described above can be added another similar to it, arranged as is shown in the figure. The child beginning with doh, lays the discs on the board in ascending order in their right position until the octave is reached : doh, re, mi, fah, soh, lah, te, doh. Then he descends the scale in the same way, returning to *doh*, but continuing to place the discs always to the right : soh, fah, mi, re, doh. In this way he forms an angle. At this point he descends again to the lower staff, te, lah, soh, fah, mi, re, doh, then he ascends again on the other side : re, mi, fah, soh, lah, te, and by forming with his two lines of discs another angle in the bass, he has completed a rhombus, " the rhombus of the notes."

After the discs have been arranged in this way, the upper staff is separated from the lower. In the lower the notes are arranged according to the bass clef. In this way the first elements of musical reading are presented to the child, reading which corresponds to *sounds* with which the child's ear is already acquainted.

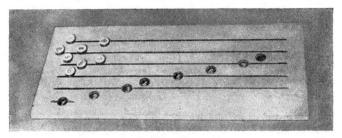

FIG. 33.

On the wooden board, round spaces are cut out corresponding to the notes.   Inside each of the spaces there is a figure. On one side of each of the discs is written a number and on the other the name of the note.   They are fitted by the child into the corresponding places.

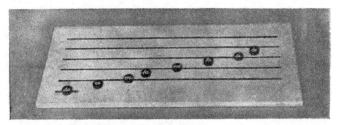

FIG. 34.

The child next arranges the discs in the notes cut out on the staff, but there are no longer numbers written to help him find the places.   Instead, he must try to remember the place of the note on the staff.   If he is not sure he consults the numbered board (Fig. 33).

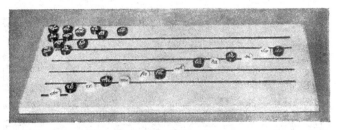

FIG. 35.

The child arranges on the staff the semitones in the spaces which remain where the discs are far apart: do-re, re-mi, fah-soh, soh-la, la-si.   The discs for the semitones have the sharp on one side and the flat on the other, e.g., re♯-mi♭ are written on the opposite sides of the same disc.

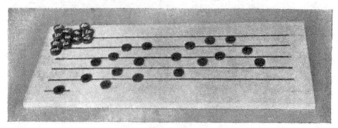

FIG. 36.

The children take a large number of discs and arrange them on the staff, leaving uppermost the side which is blank, *i.e.*, the side on which the name of the note is not written. They then verify their work by turning the discs over and reading the name.

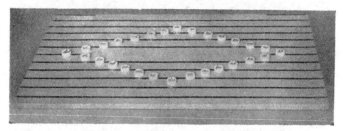

FIG. 37.

The double staff is formed by putting the two staves together. The children arrange the notes in the form of a rhombus.

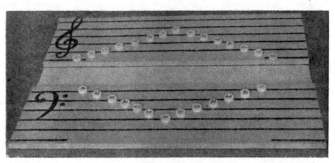

FIG. 38.

The two boards are then separated and the notes remain arranged according to the treble and bass clefs. The corresponding key signatures are then placed upon the two different staves.

For a first practical application of this knowledge we have used in our schools a miniature piano-

FIG. 39.—DUMB KEYBOARD.

forte keyboard, which reproduces the essentials
of this instrument, although in a simplified form,
and so that they are visible. Two octaves only

are reproduced, and the keys, which are small, are proportioned to the hand of a little child of four or five years, as the keys of the common piano are proportioned to those of the adult. All the mechanism of the key is visible (Fig. 39). On striking a key one sees the hammer rise, on which is written the name of the note. The hammers are black and white, like the notes.

With this instrument it is very easy for the child to practise alone, finding the notes on the keyboard corresponding to some bar of written music, and following the movements of the fingers made in playing the piano.

The keyboard in itself is mute, but a series of resonant tubes, resembling a set of organ-pipes, can be applied to the upper surface, so that the hammers striking these produce musical notes corresponding to the keys struck. The child can then pursue his exercises with the control of the musical sounds.

ARITHMETIC

The children possess all the instinctive knowledge necessary as a preparation for clear ideas on numeration. The idea of quantity was inherent in all the material for the education of the senses : longer, shorter, darker, lighter. The conceptions of identity and difference formed part of the technique of the education of the senses, which began with the recognition of identical objects, and continued with the arrangement in gradation of similar objects. I will make a special illustration of the first exercise with the solid insets, which can be done even by a child of two and a half. When he makes a mistake by putting a cylinder in a hole too large for it, and so leaves *one* cylinder without a place, he instinctively absorbs the idea of the absence of *one* from a continuous series.

The child's mind is not prepared for number by certain " preliminary ideas," given in haste by the teacher, but has been prepared for it by a process of formation, by a slow building up of itself.

To enter directly upon the teaching of arithmetic, we turn to the same didactic material used for the education of the senses.

Let us look at the three sets of material which are presented after the exercises with the solid insets, *i.e.*, the material for teaching *size* (the pink cubes), *thickness* (the brown prisms), and *length* (the green rods). There is a definite relation between the ten pieces of each series. In the material for length the shortest piece is a *unit of measurement* for all the rest ; the second piece is double the first, the third is three times the first, etc., and, whilst the scale of length increases by ten centimetres for each piece, the other dimensions remain constant (*i.e.*, the rods all have the same section).

The pieces then stand in the same relation to one another as the natural series of the numbers 1, 2, 3, 4, 5, 6, 7, 8, 9, 10.

In the second series, namely, that which shows *thickness*, whilst the length remains constant, the square section of the prisms varies. The result is that the sides of the square sections vary according to the series of natural numbers, *i.e.*, in the first prism, the square of the section has sides of one centimetre, in the second of two centimetres, in the third of three centimetres, etc., and so on, until the tenth, in which the square of the section has sides of ten centimetres. The prisms therefore are to one another as the numbers in the series of squares (1, 4, 9, 16, etc.), for it would take four prisms of the first size to make the second, nine to make the third, etc. The pieces which make up the series for teaching thickness are therefore in the following proportion : 1 : 4 : 9 : 16 : 25 : 36 : 49 : 64 : 81 : 100.

In the case of the pink cubes the edge increases

according to the numerical series, *i.e.*, the first
cube has an edge of one centimetre, the second
of two centimetres, the third of three centimetres,
and so on, to the tenth cube, which has an edge
of ten centimetres.   Hence the relation in volume
between them is that of the cubes of the series
of numbers from one to ten, *i.e.*, $1 : 8 : 27 : 64 :$
$125 : 216 : 343 : 512 : 729 : 1000$.   In fact, to make
up the volume of the second pink cube, eight of the
first little cubes would be required ; to make up
the volume of the third, twenty-seven would be
required, and so on.

The children have an intuitive knowledge of
this difference, for they realise that the exercise
with the pink cubes is the *easiest* of all three and
that with the rods the most difficult.   When we
begin the direct teaching of number, we choose
the long rods, modifying them, however, by
dividing them into ten spaces, each ten centimetres in length, coloured alternately red and
blue.   For example, the rod which is four times as
long as the first is clearly seen to be composed of
four equal lengths, red and blue ; and similarly
with all the rest.

When the rods have been placed in order of
gradation, we teach the child the numbers : one,

two, three, etc., by touching the rods in succession, from the first up to ten. Then, to help him to gain a clear idea of number, we proceed to the recognition of separate rods by means of the customary lesson in three periods.

We lay the three first rods in front of the child,

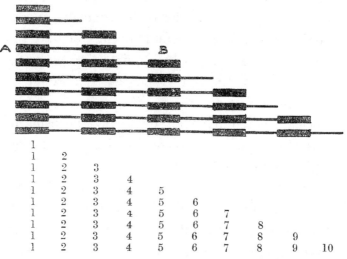

1									
1	2								
1	2	3							
1	2	3	4						
1	2	3	4	5					
1	2	3	4	5	6				
1	2	3	4	5	6	7			
1	2	3	4	5	6	7	8		
1	2	3	4	5	6	7	8	9	
1	2	3	4	5	6	7	8	9	10

FIG. 40.—DIAGRAM ILLUSTRATING USE OF NUMERICAL RODS.

and pointing to them or taking them in the hand in turn, in order to show them to him, we say: "This is *one.*" "This is *two.*" "This is *three.*" We point out with the finger the divisions in each rod, counting them so as to make sure, "one, two: this is *two.*" "One, two, three: this is *three.*" Then we say to the child : " Give me *two.*" " Give me *one.*" " Give me *three.*" Finally, pointing to a rod, we say, " What is this ? " The child answers, " Three," and we count together : " One two, three."

In the same way we teach all the other rods in their order, adding always one or two more according to the responsiveness of the child.

The importance of this didactic material is that it gives a clear idea of *number*. For when a number is named it exists as an object, a unity in itself. When we say that a man possesses a million, we mean that he has a *fortune* which is worth so many units of measure of values, and these units all belong to one person.

So, if we add 7 to 8 (7 + 8), we add a *number to a number,* and these numbers for a definite reason represent in themselves groups of homogeneous units.

Again, when the child shows us the *9,* he is handling a rod which is inflexible—an object complete in itself, composed of *nine equal parts* which can be counted. And when, after a short time, he comes to add 8 to 2, he will place next to one another, two rods, two objects, one of which has eight equal lengths and the other two.

When, on the other hand, in ordinary schools, to make the calculation easier, they present the child with objects to count, such as beans, marbles, etc., and when, to take the case I have quoted (8 + 2), he takes a group of eight marbles and adds two more marbles to it, the natural impression in his mind is not that he has added 8 to 2, but that he has added $1 + 1 + 1 + 1 + 1 + 1 + 1 + 1$ to $1 + 1$. The result is not so clear, and the child is required to make the effort of holding in his mind the idea of a group of eight objects as *one united whole*, corresponding to a single number, 8.

This effort often puts the child back, and delays his understanding of number by months or even years.

The addition and subtraction of numbers under ten are also made very much easier by the use of the didactic material for teaching lengths.   Let the child be presented with the attractive problem of arranging the pieces in such a way as to have a set of rods, all as long as the longest. He first arranges the rods in their right order (the long stair) ; he then takes the last rod (1) and lays it next to the 9. Similarly, he takes the last rod but one (2) and lays it next to the 8, and so on up to the 5.

This very simple game represents the addition of numbers within the ten : $9 + 1, 8 + 2, 7 + 3, 6 + 4$. Then, when he puts the rods back in their places, he must first take away the 4 and put it back under the 5, and then take away in their turn the 3, the 2, the 1. By this action he has put the rods back again in their right gradation, but he has also performed a series of arithmetical subtractions, $10 - 4, 10 - 3, 10 - 2, 10 - 1$.

The teaching of the figures marks a transition from the rods to the numeration of separate units. When the figures are known, *they* will serve the very purpose in the abstract which the rods serve in the concrete; that is, they will stand for the uniting into one whole of a certain number of separate units. The *synthetic* function of language and the vast field which it throws open for the operation of the intelligence is *demonstrated*, one might say, by the function of the *figure*, which now can be substituted for the concrete rods.

The use of the actual rods only would limit arithmetic to the small operations within the ten or numbers a little higher, and, in the construction of the mind, these operations would advance very little further than the limits of the first simple and elementary education of the senses. The figure, which is a word, a graphic sign, will permit of that unlimited progress which the mathematical mind of man has been able to make in the course of its evolution.

Among the didactic material there is a box containing smooth cards, on which are gummed the figures from one to nine cut out in sandpaper. These are analogous to the cards on which are gummed the sandpaper letters of the alphabet. The method of teaching is always the same. The child is taught *to touch* the figures in the sense of writing, and to name them at the same time. In this case, however, he does more than when he learned the letters ; he is shown how to place each figure upon its corresponding rod.

When all the figures have been learned in this way, one of the first exercises will be to place the number cards upon the rods arranged in gradation. So arranged, they form a succession of steps on which it is a pleasure to place the cards, and the children remain for a long time repeating this intelligent game.

After this comes what we may call the " emancipation " of the child. He carries his own figures with him, and now *using them* he will be able to group units together.   For this purpose we have in the didactic material a series of wooden pegs, but in addition to these we give the children all sorts of small objects—sticks, tiny cubes, counters, etc.

The exercise will consist in placing opposite a figure the number of objects that it indicates. The child for this purpose can use the box which

FIG. 41.—COUNTING BOXES.

is included in the material (Fig. 41).   This box is divided into compartments, above each of which is printed a figure, and the child places in the compartment the corresponding number of pegs.

Another exercise is to lay all the figures on the table and place below them the corresponding number of cubes, counters, etc.

This is only the first step, and it would be impossible here to speak of the succeeding lessons in zero, in tens and in other arithmetical processes

—for the development of which my larger works must be consulted. The didactic material itself, however, can give some idea. In the box containing the pegs there is one compartment over which the 0 is printed. Inside this compartment " nothing must be put," and then we begin with *one*.

Zero is nothing, but it is placed next to one to enable us to count when we pass beyond 9— thus, 10.

If, instead of the piece 1, we were to take pieces as long as the rod 10, we could count 10, 20, 30, 40, 50, 60, 70, 80, 90. In the didactic material there are frames containing cards on which are printed such numbers from 10 to 90. These numbers are fixed into a frame in such a way that the figures 1 to 9 can be slipped in, covering the zero. If the zero of 10 is covered by 1 the result is 11, if with 2 it becomes 12, and so on, until the last 9. Then we pass to the twenties (the second ten), and so on, from ten to ten (Fig. 42).

For the beginning of this exercise with the cards marking the tens we can use the rods. As we begin with the first ten (10) in the frame, we take the rod 10. We then place the small rod

1 next to rod 10, and at the same time slip in the number 1, covering the zero of the 10.   Then we take away rod 1, and figure 1 from the frame,

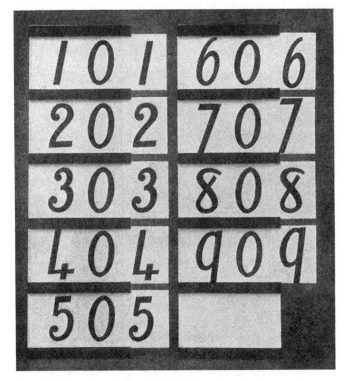

FIG. 42.

and put in their place rod 2 next to rod 10, and figure 2 over the zero in the frame, and so on, up to 9.   To advance further we should need to use two rods of 10 to make 20.

The children show much enthusiasm when learning these exercises, which demand from them two sets of activities, and give them in their work clearness of idea.

In writing and arithmetic we have gathered the fruits of a laborious education which consisted in co-ordinating the movements and gaining a first knowledge of the world. This culture comes as a natural consequence of man's first efforts to put himself into intelligent communication with the world.

All those early acquisitions, which have brought order into the child's mind, would be wasted were they not firmly established by means of written language and of figures. Thus established, however, these experiences open up an unlimited field for future education. What we have done, therefore, is to introduce the child to a higher level—the level of " culture," and he will now be able to pass on to a *school;* not, however, the school as we know it to-day, where, irrationally, we try to give culture to minds not yet prepared or *educated to receive it.*

To preserve the health of their minds, which have been *exercised* and not *fatigued* by the order of the work, our children must have a new kind of school for the acquisition of culture. My experiments in the continuation of this method for older children are already far advanced.

MORAL FACTORS

A brief description such as this, of the *means* which are used in the Children's House, may perhaps give the reader the impression of a logical and convincing system of education. But the importance of my method does not lie in the organisation itself, but *in the effects which it produces on the child.* It is the *child* who proves the value of this method by his spontaneous manifestations, which seem to reveal the laws of man's inner development.* Psychology will perhaps find in the Children's Houses a laboratory which will bring more truths to light than those hitherto recognised; for the essential factor in psychological research, especially in the field of psychogenesis, the origin and development of the mind, must be the establishment of normal conditions for the free development of thought.

As is well known, we leave the children *free* in their work, and in all actions which are not of a disturbing kind. That is, we *eliminate* disorder,

* See the chapters on Discipline in my larger works.

which is " bad," but allow to that which is orderly and " good " the most complete liberty of manifestation.

Our results have been surprising, for the children have shown a love of work which no one suspected to be in them, and have attained a calm and an orderliness in their movements which, surpassing the limits of " correctness," have entered into those of " grace." The spontaneous discipline, and the obedience which is manifested throughout the whole class, constitute the most striking result of our method.

The ancient philosophical discussion as to whether man is born good or evil is often brought forward in connection with my method, and many who have supported it have done so on the ground that it provides a demonstration of man's natural goodness. Very many others, on the contrary, have opposed it, considering that to leave children free is a dangerous mistake, since they have in them innate tendencies to evil.

I should like to put the question upon a more positive plane.

In the words " good " and " evil " we include the most varying ideas, and we confuse them especially *in our practical dealings with little children.*

The tendencies which we stigmatize as *evil* in little children of three to six years of age are often merely those which cause *annoyance* to us adults when, not understanding their needs, we try to prevent their *every movement, their every attempt to gain experience for themselves in the world* (by touching things, etc.). The child, however, through this *natural tendency*, is led to *co-ordinate his movements* and to collect impressions, especially sensations of touch, so that when prevented he *rebels*, and this rebellion forms almost the whole of his " naughtiness."

What wonder then that the *evil* disappears when, if we offer the right means for development and leave the child full liberty to use them, rebellion has no more reason for existence ?

Further, by the substitution of a series of outbursts of *joy* for the old series of outbursts of *rage*, the moral physiognomy of the child comes to assume a calm and gentleness which make him appear a different being.

It was we who provoked the children to the violent manifestations of a real *struggle for existence*. In order to exist *according to the needs of their psychic development* they had often to snatch from us the things which seemed necessary to them for the purpose. They had to move contrary to our laws, or sometimes to struggle with other children to wrest from them the objects of their desire.

On the other hand, if we give children the *means of existence*, the struggle for it disappears, and a vigorous expansion of life takes its place. This question involves a hygienic principle connected with the nervous system during the difficult period when the brain is still rapidly growing, and should be of great interest to specialists in children's diseases and nervous derangements. The inner life of man and the beginnings of his intellect are controlled by special laws and vital necessities which must not be forgotten if we are aiming at the health of mankind.

For this reason an educational method, which cultivates and protects the inner activities of the child, is not a question which is limited merely to the school and to teachers; it is a universal question which concerns the family, and is of vital interest to mothers.

To go more deeply into a question is often the only means of answering it rightly. If, for instance, we were to see men fighting over a piece

of bread, we might say : " How bad men are ! "
If, on the other hand, we entered a well-warmed
eating-house, and saw them quietly finding a place
and choosing their meal without any envy of
one another, we might say : " How good men
are ! " Evidently, the question of absolute good
and evil, intuitive ideas of which guide us in
our superficial judgment, goes beyond such limita-
tions as these. We might, for instance, provide
excellent eating-houses for an entire people without directly affecting the question of their morals.
One might say, indeed, that to judge by appear-
ances, a well-fed people are *better, quieter, and
commit less crime* than a nation that is ill-
nourished, but whoever draws from that the conclusion that to make men good it is *enough*
to feed them, will be making an obvious
mistake.

It cannot be denied, however, that *nourishment*
will be an essential factor in obtaining goodness,
in the sense that it will *eliminate* all the *evil acts,
and the bitterness of spirit* caused by the lack of
bread.

Now, in our case, we are dealing with a far
deeper need—the nourishment of man's inner
life, and of his higher functions. The bread we

are dealing with is the bread of the spirit, and we are entering into the difficult subject of the satis- faction of man's psychic needs.

We have already obtained a most interesting result, in that we have found it possible to present *new means* of enabling children to reach a higher level of calm and goodness, and we have been able to establish these means by experience. The whole foundation of our results rests upon these means which we have discovered, and which may be divided under two heads—the *organisation of work,* and liberty.

It is the perfect organisation of work, permitting the possibility of self-development and giving outlet for the energies, which procures for each child the beneficial and calming *satisfaction.* And it is under such conditions of work that liberty leads to a perfecting of the activities, and to the attainment of a fine discipline which is in itself the result of that new quality of *calmness* that has been developed in the child.

Freedom without organisation of work would be useless. The child left *free* without means of work would go to waste, just as a new-born baby, if *left free* without nourishment, would die of star- vation. *The organisation of the work,* therefore, is the corner-stone of this new structure of goodness; but even that organisation would be in vain without the *liberty* to make use of it, and without freedom for the expansion of all those energies which spring from the satisfaction of the child's highest activities.

Has not a similar phenomenon occurred also in the history of man ? The history of civilisation is a history of successful attempts to organise work and to obtain liberty. On the whole, man's goodness has also increased, as is shown by his progress from barbarism to civilisation, and it may be said that crime, the various forms of wickedness, cruelty and violence have been gradually decreasing during this passage of time.

The *criminality* of our times, as a matter of fact, has been compared to a form of *barbarism* surviving in the midst of civilised peoples. It is therefore, through the better organisation of work that society will probably attain to a further purification ; and in the meanwhile it seems unconsciously to be seeking the overthrow of the last barriers between itself and liberty.

If this is what we learn from society, how great should be the results among little children of three to six years of age if the organisation of their

work is complete, and their freedom absolute ?
It is for this reason that to us they seem so good;
like heralds of hope and of redemption.

If men, walking as yet so painfully and imper-
fectly along the road of work and of freedom, have
become better, why should we fear that the same
road will prove disastrous to the children ?

Yet, on the other hand, I would not say that
the goodness of our little ones in their freedom
will solve the problem of the absolute goodness
or wickedness of man.   We can only say that we
have made a contribution to the cause of goodness
by removing obstacles which were the cause of
violence and of rebellion.

Let us "render, therefore, unto Cæsar the
things that are Cæsar's, and unto God the things
that are God's."

A CATALOG OF SELECTED
DOVER BOOKS
IN ALL FIELDS OF INTEREST

A CATALOG OF SELECTED DOVER
BOOKS IN ALL FIELDS OF INTEREST

100 BEST-LOVED POEMS, Edited by Philip Smith. "The Passionate Shepherd to His Love," "Shall I compare thee to a summer's day?" "Death, be not proud," "The Raven," "The Road Not Taken," plus works by Blake, Wordsworth, Byron, Shelley, Keats, many others. 96pp. 5³⁄₁₆ x 8¼.   0-486-28553-7

100 SMALL HOUSES OF THE THIRTIES, Brown-Blodgett Company. Exterior photographs and floor plans for 100 charming structures. Illustrations of models accompanied by descriptions of interiors, color schemes, closet space, and other amenities. 200 illustrations. 112pp. 8⅜ x 11.   0-486-44131-8

1000 TURN-OF-THE-CENTURY HOUSES: With Illustrations and Floor Plans, Herbert C. Chivers. Reproduced from a rare edition, this showcase of homes ranges from cottages and bungalows to sprawling mansions. Each house is meticulously illustrated and accompanied by complete floor plans. 256pp. 9⅜ x 12¼.

0-486-45596-3

101 GREAT AMERICAN POEMS, Edited by The American Poetry & Literacy Project. Rich treasury of verse from the 19th and 20th centuries includes works by Edgar Allan Poe, Robert Frost, Walt Whitman, Langston Hughes, Emily Dickinson, T. S. Eliot, other notables. 96pp. 5³⁄₁₆ x 8¼.   0-486-40158-8

101 GREAT SAMURAI PRINTS, Utagawa Kuniyoshi. Kuniyoshi was a master of the warrior woodblock print — and these 18th-century illustrations represent the pinnacle of his craft. Full-color portraits of renowned Japanese samurais pulse with movement, passion, and remarkably fine detail. 112pp. 8⅜ x 11.   0-486-46523-3

ABC OF BALLET, Janet Grosser. Clearly worded, abundantly illustrated little guide defines basic ballet-related terms: arabesque, battement, pas de chat, relevé, sissonne, many others. Pronunciation guide included. Excellent primer. 48pp. 4³⁄₁₆ x 5¾.

0-486-40871-X

ACCESSORIES OF DRESS: An Illustrated Encyclopedia, Katherine Lester and Bess Viola Oerke. Illustrations of hats, veils, wigs, cravats, shawls, shoes, gloves, and other accessories enhance an engaging commentary that reveals the humor and charm of the many-sided story of accessorized apparel. 644 figures and 59 plates. 608pp. 6⅛ x 9¼.

0-486-43378-1

ADVENTURES OF HUCKLEBERRY FINN, Mark Twain. Join Huck and Jim as their boyhood adventures along the Mississippi River lead them into a world of excitement, danger, and self-discovery. Humorous narrative, lyrical descriptions of the Mississippi valley, and memorable characters. 224pp. 5³⁄₁₆ x 8¼.   0-486-28061-6

ALICE STARMORE'S BOOK OF FAIR ISLE KNITTING, Alice Starmore. A noted designer from the region of Scotland's Fair Isle explores the history and techniques of this distinctive, stranded-color knitting style and provides copious illustrated instructions for 14 original knitwear designs. 208pp. 8⅜ x 10⅞.   0-486-47218-3

ALICE'S ADVENTURES IN WONDERLAND, Lewis Carroll. Beloved classic about a little girl lost in a topsy-turvy land and her encounters with the White Rabbit, March Hare, Mad Hatter, Cheshire Cat, and other delightfully improbable characters. 42 illustrations by Sir John Tenniel. 96pp. 5³⁄₁₆ x 8¼. 0-486-27543-4

AMERICA'S LIGHTHOUSES: An Illustrated History, Francis Ross Holland. Profusely illustrated fact-filled survey of American lighthouses since 1716. Over 200 stations — East, Gulf, and West coasts, Great Lakes, Hawaii, Alaska, Puerto Rico, the Virgin Islands, and the Mississippi and St. Lawrence Rivers. 240pp. 8 x 10¾.
0-486-25576-X

AN ENCYCLOPEDIA OF THE VIOLIN, Alberto Bachmann. Translated by Frederick H. Martens. Introduction by Eugene Ysaye. First published in 1925, this renowned reference remains unsurpassed as a source of essential information, from construction and evolution to repertoire and technique. Includes a glossary and 73 illustrations. 496pp. 6½ x 9¼. 0-486-46618-3

ANIMALS: 1,419 Copyright-Free Illustrations of Mammals, Birds, Fish, Insects, etc., Selected by Jim Harter. Selected for its visual impact and ease of use, this outstanding collection of wood engravings presents over 1,000 species of animals in extremely lifelike poses. Includes mammals, birds, reptiles, amphibians, fish, insects, and other invertebrates. 284pp. 9 x 12. 0-486-23766-4

THE ANNALS, Tacitus. Translated by Alfred John Church and William Jackson Brodribb. This vital chronicle of Imperial Rome, written by the era's great historian, spans A.D. 14-68 and paints incisive psychological portraits of major figures, from Tiberius to Nero. 416pp. 5³⁄₁₆ x 8¼. 0-486-45236-0

ANTIGONE, Sophocles. Filled with passionate speeches and sensitive probing of moral and philosophical issues, this powerful and often-performed Greek drama reveals the grim fate that befalls the children of Oedipus. Footnotes. 64pp. 5³⁄₁₆ x 8 ¼. 0-486-27804-2

ART DECO DECORATIVE PATTERNS IN FULL COLOR, Christian Stoll. Reprinted from a rare 1910 portfolio, 160 sensuous and exotic images depict a breathtaking array of florals, geometrics, and abstracts — all elegant in their stark simplicity. 64pp. 8⅜ x 11. 0-486-44862-2

THE ARTHUR RACKHAM TREASURY: 86 Full-Color Illustrations, Arthur Rackham. Selected and Edited by Jeff A. Menges. A stunning treasury of 86 full-page plates span the famed English artist's career, from *Rip Van Winkle* (1905) to masterworks such as *Undine, A Midsummer Night's Dream,* and *Wind in the Willows* (1939). 96pp. 8⅜ x 11.
0-486-44685-9

THE AUTHENTIC GILBERT & SULLIVAN SONGBOOK, W. S. Gilbert and A. S. Sullivan. The most comprehensive collection available, this songbook includes selections from every one of Gilbert and Sullivan's light operas. Ninety-two numbers are presented uncut and unedited, and in their original keys. 410pp. 9 x 12.
0-486-23482-7

THE AWAKENING, Kate Chopin. First published in 1899, this controversial novel of a New Orleans wife's search for love outside a stifling marriage shocked readers. Today, it remains a first-rate narrative with superb characterization. New introductory Note. 128pp. 5³⁄₁₆ x 8¼. 0-486-27786-0

BASIC DRAWING, Louis Priscilla. Beginning with perspective, this commonsense manual progresses to the figure in movement, light and shade, anatomy, drapery, composition, trees and landscape, and outdoor sketching. Black-and-white illustrations throughout. 128pp. 8⅜ x 11. 0-486-45815-6

THE BATTLES THAT CHANGED HISTORY, Fletcher Pratt. Historian profiles 16 crucial conflicts, ancient to modern, that changed the course of Western civilization. Gripping accounts of battles led by Alexander the Great, Joan of Arc, Ulysses S. Grant, other commanders. 27 maps. 352pp. 5⅜ x 8½. 0-486-41129-X

BEETHOVEN'S LETTERS, Ludwig van Beethoven. Edited by Dr. A. C. Kalischer. Features 457 letters to fellow musicians, friends, greats, patrons, and literary men. Reveals musical thoughts, quirks of personality, insights, and daily events. Includes 15 plates. 410pp. 5⅜ x 8½. 0-486-22769-3

BERNICE BOBS HER HAIR AND OTHER STORIES, F. Scott Fitzgerald. This brilliant anthology includes 6 of Fitzgerald's most popular stories: "The Diamond as Big as the Ritz," the title tale, "The Offshore Pirate," "The Ice Palace," "The Jelly Bean," and "May Day." 176pp. 5⅜ x 8½. 0-486-47049-0

BESLER'S BOOK OF FLOWERS AND PLANTS: 73 Full-Color Plates from Hortus Eystettensis, 1613, Basilius Besler. Here is a selection of magnificent plates from the *Hortus Eystettensis,* which vividly illustrated and identified the plants, flowers, and trees that thrived in the legendary German garden at Eichstätt. 80pp. 8⅜ x 11. 0-486-46005-3

THE BOOK OF KELLS, Edited by Blanche Cirker. Painstakingly reproduced from a rare facsimile edition, this volume contains full-page decorations, portraits, illustrations, plus a sampling of textual leaves with exquisite calligraphy and ornamentation. 32 full-color illustrations. 32pp. 9⅜ x 12¼. 0-486-24345-1

THE BOOK OF THE CROSSBOW: With an Additional Section on Catapults and Other Siege Engines, Ralph Payne-Gallwey. Fascinating study traces history and use of crossbow as military and sporting weapon, from Middle Ages to modern times. Also covers related weapons: balistas, catapults, Turkish bows, more. Over 240 illustrations. 400pp. 7¼ x 10⅛. 0-486-28720-3

THE BUNGALOW BOOK: Floor Plans and Photos of 112 Houses, 1910, Henry L. Wilson. Here are 112 of the most popular and economic blueprints of the early 20th century — plus an illustration or photograph of each completed house. A wonderful time capsule that still offers a wealth of valuable insights. 160pp. 8⅜ x 11. 0-486-45104-6

THE CALL OF THE WILD, Jack London. A classic novel of adventure, drawn from London's own experiences as a Klondike adventurer, relating the story of a heroic dog caught in the brutal life of the Alaska Gold Rush. Note. 64pp. 5 3/16 x 8¼. 0-486-26472-6

CANDIDE, Voltaire. Edited by Francois-Marie Arouet. One of the world's great satires since its first publication in 1759. Witty, caustic skewering of romance, science, philosophy, religion, government — nearly all human ideals and institutions. 112pp. 5 3/16 x 8¼. 0-486-26689-3

CELEBRATED IN THEIR TIME: Photographic Portraits from the George Grantham Bain Collection, Edited by Amy Pastan. With an Introduction by Michael Carlebach. Remarkable portrait gallery features 112 rare images of Albert Einstein, Charlie Chaplin, the Wright Brothers, Henry Ford, and other luminaries from the worlds of politics, art, entertainment, and industry. 128pp. 8⅜ x 11. 0-486-46754-6

CHARIOTS FOR APOLLO: The NASA History of Manned Lunar Spacecraft to 1969, Courtney G. Brooks, James M. Grimwood, and Loyd S. Swenson, Jr. This illustrated history by a trio of experts is the definitive reference on the Apollo spacecraft and lunar modules. It traces the vehicles' design, development, and operation in space. More than 100 photographs and illustrations. 576pp. 6¾ x 9¼. 0-486-46756-2

A CHRISTMAS CAROL, Charles Dickens. This engrossing tale relates Ebenezer Scrooge's ghostly journeys through Christmases past, present, and future and his ultimate transformation from a harsh and grasping old miser to a charitable and compassionate human being. 80pp. 5³⁄₁₆ x 8¼. 0-486-26865-9

COMMON SENSE, Thomas Paine. First published in January of 1776, this highly influential landmark document clearly and persuasively argued for American separation from Great Britain and paved the way for the Declaration of Independence. 64pp. 5³⁄₁₆ x 8¼. 0-486-29602-4

THE COMPLETE SHORT STORIES OF OSCAR WILDE, Oscar Wilde. Complete texts of "The Happy Prince and Other Tales," "A House of Pomegranates," "Lord Arthur Savile's Crime and Other Stories," "Poems in Prose," and "The Portrait of Mr. W. H." 208pp. 5³⁄₁₆ x 8¼. 0-486-45216-6

COMPLETE SONNETS, William Shakespeare. Over 150 exquisite poems deal with love, friendship, the tyranny of time, beauty's evanescence, death, and other themes in language of remarkable power, precision, and beauty. Glossary of archaic terms. 80pp. 5³⁄₁₆ x 8¼. 0-486-26686-9

THE COUNT OF MONTE CRISTO: Abridged Edition, Alexandre Dumas. Falsely accused of treason, Edmond Dantès is imprisoned in the bleak Chateau d'If. After a hair-raising escape, he launches an elaborate plot to extract a bitter revenge against those who betrayed him. 448pp. 5³⁄₁₆ x 8¼. 0-486-45643-9

CRAFTSMAN BUNGALOWS: Designs from the Pacific Northwest, Yoho & Merritt. This reprint of a rare catalog, showcasing the charming simplicity and cozy style of Craftsman bungalows, is filled with photos of completed homes, plus floor plans and estimated costs. An indispensable resource for architects, historians, and illustrators. 112pp. 10 x 7. 0-486-46875-5

CRAFTSMAN BUNGALOWS: 59 Homes from "The Craftsman," Edited by Gustav Stickley. Best and most attractive designs from Arts and Crafts Movement publication — 1903–1916 — includes sketches, photographs of homes, floor plans, descriptive text. 128pp. 8¼ x 11. 0-486-25829-7

CRIME AND PUNISHMENT, Fyodor Dostoyevsky. Translated by Constance Garnett. Supreme masterpiece tells the story of Raskolnikov, a student tormented by his own thoughts after he murders an old woman. Overwhelmed by guilt and terror, he confesses and goes to prison. 480pp. 5³⁄₁₆ x 8¼. 0-486-41587-2

THE DECLARATION OF INDEPENDENCE AND OTHER GREAT DOCUMENTS OF AMERICAN HISTORY: 1775-1865, Edited by John Grafton. Thirteen compelling and influential documents: Henry's "Give Me Liberty or Give Me Death," Declaration of Independence, The Constitution, Washington's First Inaugural Address, The Monroe Doctrine, The Emancipation Proclamation, Gettysburg Address, more. 64pp. 5³⁄₁₆ x 8¼. 0-486-41124-9

THE DESERT AND THE SOWN: Travels in Palestine and Syria, Gertrude Bell. "The female Lawrence of Arabia," Gertrude Bell wrote captivating, perceptive accounts of her travels in the Middle East. This intriguing narrative, accompanied by 160 photos, traces her 1905 sojourn in Lebanon, Syria, and Palestine. 368pp. 5⅜ x 8½. 0-486-46876-3

A DOLL'S HOUSE, Henrik Ibsen. Ibsen's best-known play displays his genius for realistic prose drama. An expression of women's rights, the play climaxes when the central character, Nora, rejects a smothering marriage and life in "a doll's house." 80pp. 5³⁄₁₆ x 8¼. 0-486-27062-9

DOOMED SHIPS: Great Ocean Liner Disasters, William H. Miller, Jr. Nearly 200 photographs, many from private collections, highlight tales of some of the vessels whose pleasure cruises ended in catastrophe: the *Morro Castle, Normandie, Andrea Doria, Europa,* and many others. 128pp. 8⅞ x 11¾. 0-486-45366-9

THE DORÉ BIBLE ILLUSTRATIONS, Gustave Doré. Detailed plates from the Bible: the Creation scenes, Adam and Eve, horrifying visions of the Flood, the battle sequences with their monumental crowds, depictions of the life of Jesus, 241 plates in all. 241pp. 9 x 12. 0-486-23004-X

DRAWING DRAPERY FROM HEAD TO TOE, Cliff Young. Expert guidance on how to draw shirts, pants, skirts, gloves, hats, and coats on the human figure, including folds in relation to the body, pull and crush, action folds, creases, more. Over 200 drawings. 48pp. 8¼ x 11. 0-486-45591-2

DUBLINERS, James Joyce. A fine and accessible introduction to the work of one of the 20th century's most influential writers, this collection features 15 tales, including a masterpiece of the short-story genre, "The Dead." 160pp. 5³⁄₁₆ x 8¼.
0-486-26870-5

EASY-TO-MAKE POP-UPS, Joan Irvine. Illustrated by Barbara Reid. Dozens of wonderful ideas for three-dimensional paper fun — from holiday greeting cards with moving parts to a pop-up menagerie. Easy-to-follow, illustrated instructions for more than 30 projects. 299 black-and-white illustrations. 96pp. 8⅜ x 11.
0-486-44622-0

EASY-TO-MAKE STORYBOOK DOLLS: A "Novel" Approach to Cloth Dollmaking, Sherralyn St. Clair. Favorite fictional characters come alive in this unique beginner's dollmaking guide. Includes patterns for Pollyanna, Dorothy from *The Wonderful Wizard of Oz,* Mary of *The Secret Garden,* plus easy-to-follow instructions, 263 black-and-white illustrations, and an 8-page color insert. 112pp. 8¼ x 11. 0-486-47360-0

EINSTEIN'S ESSAYS IN SCIENCE, Albert Einstein. Speeches and essays in accessible, everyday language profile influential physicists such as Niels Bohr and Isaac Newton. They also explore areas of physics to which the author made major contributions. 128pp. 5 x 8. 0-486-47011-3

EL DORADO: Further Adventures of the Scarlet Pimpernel, Baroness Orczy. A popular sequel to *The Scarlet Pimpernel,* this suspenseful story recounts the Pimpernel's attempts to rescue the Dauphin from imprisonment during the French Revolution. An irresistible blend of intrigue, period detail, and vibrant characterizations. 352pp. 5³⁄₁₆ x 8¼. 0-486-44026-5

ELEGANT SMALL HOMES OF THE TWENTIES: 99 Designs from a Competition, Chicago Tribune. Nearly 100 designs for five- and six-room houses feature New England and Southern colonials, Normandy cottages, stately Italianate dwellings, and other fascinating snapshots of American domestic architecture of the 1920s. 112pp. 9 x 12. 0-486-46910-7

THE ELEMENTS OF STYLE: The Original Edition, William Strunk, Jr. This is the book that generations of writers have relied upon for timeless advice on grammar, diction, syntax, and other essentials. In concise terms, it identifies the principal requirements of proper style and common errors. 64pp. 5⅜ x 8½. 0-486-44798-7

THE ELUSIVE PIMPERNEL, Baroness Orczy. Robespierre's revolutionaries find their wicked schemes thwarted by the heroic Pimpernel — Sir Percival Blakeney. In this thrilling sequel, Chauvelin devises a plot to eliminate the Pimpernel and his wife. 272pp. 5³⁄₁₆ x 8¼. 0-486-45464-9

Browse over 9,000 books at www.doverpublications.com

AN ENCYCLOPEDIA OF BATTLES: Accounts of Over 1,560 Battles from 1479 B.C. to the Present, David Eggenberger. Essential details of every major battle in recorded history from the first battle of Megiddo in 1479 B.C. to Grenada in 1984. List of battle maps. 99 illustrations. 544pp. 6½ x 9¼. 0-486-24913-1

ENCYCLOPEDIA OF EMBROIDERY STITCHES, INCLUDING CREWEL, Marion Nichols. Precise explanations and instructions, clearly illustrated, on how to work chain, back, cross, knotted, woven stitches, and many more — 178 in all, including Cable Outline, Whipped Satin, and Eyelet Buttonhole. Over 1400 illustrations. 219pp. 8⅜ x 11¼. 0-486-22929-7

ENTER JEEVES: 15 Early Stories, P. G. Wodehouse. Splendid collection contains first 8 stories featuring Bertie Wooster, the deliciously dim aristocrat and Jeeves, his brainy, imperturbable manservant. Also, the complete Reggie Pepper (Bertie's prototype) series. 288pp. 5⅜ x 8½. 0-486-29717-9

ERIC SLOANE'S AMERICA: Paintings in Oil, Michael Wigley. With a Foreword by Mimi Sloane. Eric Sloane's evocative oils of America's landscape and material culture shimmer with immense historical and nostalgic appeal. This original hardcover collection gathers nearly a hundred of his finest paintings, with subjects ranging from New England to the American Southwest. 128pp. 10⅝ x 9. 0-486-46525-X

ETHAN FROME, Edith Wharton. Classic story of wasted lives, set against a bleak New England background. Superbly delineated characters in a hauntingly grim tale of thwarted love. Considered by many to be Wharton's masterpiece. 96pp. 5³⁄₁₆ x 8 ¼. 0-486-26690-7

THE EVERLASTING MAN, G. K. Chesterton. Chesterton's view of Christianity — as a blend of philosophy and mythology, satisfying intellect and spirit — applies to his brilliant book, which appeals to readers' heads as well as their hearts. 288pp. 5⅜ x 8½. 0-486-46036-3

THE FIELD AND FOREST HANDY BOOK, Daniel Beard. Written by a co-founder of the Boy Scouts, this appealing guide offers illustrated instructions for building kites, birdhouses, boats, igloos, and other fun projects, plus numerous helpful tips for campers. 448pp. 5³⁄₁₆ x 8¼. 0-486-46191-2

FINDING YOUR WAY WITHOUT MAP OR COMPASS, Harold Gatty. Useful, instructive manual shows would-be explorers, hikers, bikers, scouts, sailors, and survivalists how to find their way outdoors by observing animals, weather patterns, shifting sands, and other elements of nature. 288pp. 5⅜ x 8½. 0-486-40613-X

FIRST FRENCH READER: A Beginner's Dual-Language Book, Edited and Translated by Stanley Appelbaum. This anthology introduces 50 legendary writers — Voltaire, Balzac, Baudelaire, Proust, more — through passages from *The Red and the Black, Les Misérables, Madame Bovary,* and other classics. Original French text plus English translation on facing pages. 240pp. 5⅜ x 8½. 0-486-46178-5

FIRST GERMAN READER: A Beginner's Dual-Language Book, Edited by Harry Steinhauer. Specially chosen for their power to evoke German life and culture, these short, simple readings include poems, stories, essays, and anecdotes by Goethe, Hesse, Heine, Schiller, and others. 224pp. 5⅜ x 8½. 0-486-46179-3

FIRST SPANISH READER: A Beginner's Dual-Language Book, Angel Flores. Delightful stories, other material based on works of Don Juan Manuel, Luis Taboada, Ricardo Palma, other noted writers. Complete faithful English translations on facing pages. Exercises. 176pp. 5⅜ x 8½. 0-486-25810-6

Browse over 9,000 books at www.doverpublications.com

FIVE ACRES AND INDEPENDENCE, Maurice G. Kains. Great back-to-the-land classic explains basics of self-sufficient farming. The one book to get. 95 illustrations. 397pp. 5⅜ x 8½. 0-486-20974-1

FLAGG'S SMALL HOUSES: Their Economic Design and Construction, 1922, Ernest Flagg. Although most famous for his skyscrapers, Flagg was also a proponent of the well-designed single-family dwelling. His classic treatise features innovations that save space, materials, and cost. 526 illustrations. 160pp. 9⅜ x 12¼.
0-486-45197-6

FLATLAND: A Romance of Many Dimensions, Edwin A. Abbott. Classic of science (and mathematical) fiction — charmingly illustrated by the author — describes the adventures of A. Square, a resident of Flatland, in Spaceland (three dimensions), Lineland (one dimension), and Pointland (no dimensions). 96pp. 5³⁄₁₆ x 8¼.
0-486-27263-X

FRANKENSTEIN, Mary Shelley. The story of Victor Frankenstein's monstrous creation and the havoc it caused has enthralled generations of readers and inspired countless writers of horror and suspense. With the author's own 1831 introduction. 176pp. 5³⁄₁₆ x 8¼. 0-486-28211-2

THE GARGOYLE BOOK: 572 Examples from Gothic Architecture, Lester Burbank Bridaham. Dispelling the conventional wisdom that French Gothic architectural flourishes were born of despair or gloom, Bridaham reveals the whimsical nature of these creations and the ingenious artisans who made them. 572 illustrations. 224pp. 8⅜ x 11. 0-486-44754-5

THE GIFT OF THE MAGI AND OTHER SHORT STORIES, O. Henry. Sixteen captivating stories by one of America's most popular storytellers. Included are such classics as "The Gift of the Magi," "The Last Leaf," and "The Ransom of Red Chief." Publisher's Note. 96pp. 5³⁄₁₆ x 8¼. 0-486-27061-0

THE GOETHE TREASURY: Selected Prose and Poetry, Johann Wolfgang von Goethe. Edited, Selected, and with an Introduction by Thomas Mann. In addition to his lyric poetry, Goethe wrote travel sketches, autobiographical studies, essays, letters, and proverbs in rhyme and prose. This collection presents outstanding examples from each genre. 368pp. 5⅜ x 8½. 0-486-44780-4

GREAT EXPECTATIONS, Charles Dickens. Orphaned Pip is apprenticed to the dirty work of the forge but dreams of becoming a gentleman — and one day finds himself in possession of "great expectations." Dickens' finest novel. 400pp. 5³⁄₁₆ x 8¼.
0-486-41586-4

GREAT WRITERS ON THE ART OF FICTION: From Mark Twain to Joyce Carol Oates, Edited by James Daley. An indispensable source of advice and inspiration, this anthology features essays by Henry James, Kate Chopin, Willa Cather, Sinclair Lewis, Jack London, Raymond Chandler, Raymond Carver, Eudora Welty, and Kurt Vonnegut, Jr. 192pp. 5⅜ x 8½. 0-486-45128-3

HAMLET, William Shakespeare. The quintessential Shakespearean tragedy, whose highly charged confrontations and anguished soliloquies probe depths of human feeling rarely sounded in any art. Reprinted from an authoritative British edition complete with illuminating footnotes. 128pp. 5³⁄₁₆ x 8¼. 0-486-27278-8

THE HAUNTED HOUSE, Charles Dickens. A Yuletide gathering in an eerie country retreat provides the backdrop for Dickens and his friends — including Elizabeth Gaskell and Wilkie Collins — who take turns spinning supernatural yarns. 144pp. 5⅜ x 8½. 0-486-46309-5

HEART OF DARKNESS, Joseph Conrad. Dark allegory of a journey up the Congo River and the narrator's encounter with the mysterious Mr. Kurtz. Masterly blend of adventure, character study, psychological penetration. For many, Conrad's finest, most enigmatic story. 80pp. 5³⁄₁₆ x 8¼.   0-486-26464-5

HENSON AT THE NORTH POLE, Matthew A. Henson. This thrilling memoir by the heroic African-American who was Peary's companion through two decades of Arctic exploration recounts a tale of danger, courage, and determination. "Fascinating and exciting." — *Commonweal.* 128pp. 5⅜ x 8½.   0-486-45472-X

HISTORIC COSTUMES AND HOW TO MAKE THEM, Mary Fernald and E. Shenton. Practical, informative guidebook shows how to create everything from short tunics worn by Saxon men in the fifth century to a lady's bustle dress of the late 1800s. 81 illustrations. 176pp. 5⅜ x 8½.   0-486-44906-8

THE HOUND OF THE BASKERVILLES, Arthur Conan Doyle. A deadly curse in the form of a legendary ferocious beast continues to claim its victims from the Baskerville family until Holmes and Watson intervene. Often called the best detective story ever written. 128pp. 5³⁄₁₆ x 8¼.   0-486-28214-7

THE HOUSE BEHIND THE CEDARS, Charles W. Chesnutt. Originally published in 1900, this groundbreaking novel by a distinguished African-American author recounts the drama of a brother and sister who "pass for white" during the dangerous days of Reconstruction. 208pp. 5⅜ x 8½.   0-486-46144-0

THE HUMAN FIGURE IN MOTION, Eadweard Muybridge. The 4,789 photographs in this definitive selection show the human figure — models almost all undraped — engaged in over 160 different types of action: running, climbing stairs, etc. 390pp. 7⅞ x 10⅝.   0-486-20204-6

THE IMPORTANCE OF BEING EARNEST, Oscar Wilde. Wilde's witty and buoyant comedy of manners, filled with some of literature's most famous epigrams, reprinted from an authoritative British edition. Considered Wilde's most perfect work. 64pp. 5³⁄₁₆ x 8¼.   0-486-26478-5

THE INFERNO, Dante Alighieri. Translated and with notes by Henry Wadsworth Longfellow. The first stop on Dante's famous journey from Hell to Purgatory to Paradise, this 14th-century allegorical poem blends vivid and shocking imagery with graceful lyricism. Translated by the beloved 19th-century poet, Henry Wadsworth Longfellow. 256pp. 5³⁄₁₆ x 8¼.   0-486-44288-8

JANE EYRE, Charlotte Brontë. Written in 1847, *Jane Eyre* tells the tale of an orphan girl's progress from the custody of cruel relatives to an oppressive boarding school and its culmination in a troubled career as a governess. 448pp. 5³⁄₁₆ x 8¼.
0-486-42449-9

JAPANESE WOODBLOCK FLOWER PRINTS, Tanigami Kônan. Extraordinary collection of Japanese woodblock prints by a well-known artist features 120 plates in brilliant color. Realistic images from a rare edition include daffodils, tulips, and other familiar and unusual flowers. 128pp. 11 x 8¼.   0-486-46442-3

JEWELRY MAKING AND DESIGN, Augustus F. Rose and Antonio Cirino. Professional secrets of jewelry making are revealed in a thorough, practical guide. Over 200 illustrations. 306pp. 5⅜ x 8½.   0-486-21750-7

JULIUS CAESAR, William Shakespeare. Great tragedy based on Plutarch's account of the lives of Brutus, Julius Caesar and Mark Antony. Evil plotting, ringing oratory, high tragedy with Shakespeare's incomparable insight, dramatic power. Explanatory footnotes. 96pp. 5³⁄₁₆ x 8¼.   0-486-26876-4

Browse over 9,000 books at www.doverpublications.com

THE JUNGLE, Upton Sinclair. 1906 bestseller shockingly reveals intolerable labor practices and working conditions in the Chicago stockyards as it tells the grim story of a Slavic family that emigrates to America full of optimism but soon faces despair. 320pp. 5³⁄₁₆ x 8¼. 0-486-41923-1

THE KINGDOM OF GOD IS WITHIN YOU, Leo Tolstoy. The soul-searching book that inspired Gandhi to embrace the concept of passive resistance, Tolstoy's 1894 polemic clearly outlines a radical, well-reasoned revision of traditional Christian thinking. 352pp. 5³⁄₁₆ x 8¼. 0-486-45138-0

THE LADY OR THE TIGER?: and Other Logic Puzzles, Raymond M. Smullyan. Created by a renowned puzzle master, these whimsically themed challenges involve paradoxes about probability, time, and change; metapuzzles; and self-referentiality. Nineteen chapters advance in difficulty from relatively simple to highly complex. 1982 edition. 240pp. 5⅜ x 8½. 0-486-47027-X

LEAVES OF GRASS: The Original 1855 Edition, Walt Whitman. Whitman's immortal collection includes some of the greatest poems of modern times, including his masterpiece, "Song of Myself." Shattering standard conventions, it stands as an unabashed celebration of body and nature. 128pp. 5³⁄₁₆ x 8¼. 0-486-45676-5

LES MISÉRABLES, Victor Hugo. Translated by Charles E. Wilbour. Abridged by James K. Robinson. A convict's heroic struggle for justice and redemption plays out against a fiery backdrop of the Napoleonic wars. This edition features the excellent original translation and a sensitive abridgment. 304pp. 6⅛ x 9¼. 0-486-45789-3

LILITH: A Romance, George MacDonald. In this novel by the father of fantasy literature, a man travels through time to meet Adam and Eve and to explore humanity's fall from grace and ultimate redemption. 240pp. 5⅜ x 8½. 0-486-46818-6

THE LOST LANGUAGE OF SYMBOLISM, Harold Bayley. This remarkable book reveals the hidden meaning behind familiar images and words, from the origins of Santa Claus to the fleur-de-lys, drawing from mythology, folklore, religious texts, and fairy tales. 1,418 illustrations. 784pp. 5⅜ x 8½. 0-486-44787-1

MACBETH, William Shakespeare. A Scottish nobleman murders the king in order to succeed to the throne. Tortured by his conscience and fearful of discovery, he becomes tangled in a web of treachery and deceit that ultimately spells his doom. 96pp. 5³⁄₁₆ x 8¼. 0-486-27802-6

MAKING AUTHENTIC CRAFTSMAN FURNITURE: Instructions and Plans for 62 Projects, Gustav Stickley. Make authentic reproductions of handsome, functional, durable furniture: tables, chairs, wall cabinets, desks, a hall tree, and more. Construction plans with drawings, schematics, dimensions, and lumber specs reprinted from 1900s *The Craftsman* magazine. 128pp. 8⅛ x 11. 0-486-25000-8

MATHEMATICS FOR THE NONMATHEMATICIAN, Morris Kline. Erudite and entertaining overview follows development of mathematics from ancient Greeks to present. Topics include logic and mathematics, the fundamental concept, differential calculus, probability theory, much more. Exercises and problems. 641pp. 5⅜ x 8½. 0-486-24823-2

MEMOIRS OF AN ARABIAN PRINCESS FROM ZANZIBAR, Emily Ruete. This 19th-century autobiography offers a rare inside look at the society surrounding a sultan's palace. A real-life princess in exile recalls her vanished world of harems, slave trading, and court intrigues. 288pp. 5⅜ x 8½. 0-486-47121-7

THE METAMORPHOSIS AND OTHER STORIES, Franz Kafka. Excellent new English translations of title story (considered by many critics Kafka's most perfect work), plus "The Judgment," "In the Penal Colony," "A Country Doctor," and "A Report to an Academy." Note. 96pp. 5³⁄₁₆ x 8¼. 0-486-29030-1

MICROSCOPIC ART FORMS FROM THE PLANT WORLD, R. Anheisser. From undulating curves to complex geometrics, a world of fascinating images abound in this classic, illustrated survey of microscopic plants. Features 400 detailed illustrations of nature's minute but magnificent handiwork. The accompanying CD-ROM includes all of the images in the book. 128pp. 9 x 9. 0-486-46013-4

A MIDSUMMER NIGHT'S DREAM, William Shakespeare. Among the most popular of Shakespeare's comedies, this enchanting play humorously celebrates the vagaries of love as it focuses upon the intertwined romances of several pairs of lovers. Explanatory footnotes. 80pp. 5³⁄₁₆ x 8¼. 0-486-27067-X

THE MONEY CHANGERS, Upton Sinclair. Originally published in 1908, this cautionary novel from the author of *The Jungle* explores corruption within the American system as a group of power brokers joins forces for personal gain, triggering a crash on Wall Street. 192pp. 5⅜ x 8½. 0-486-46917-4

THE MOST POPULAR HOMES OF THE TWENTIES, William A. Radford. With a New Introduction by Daniel D. Reiff. Based on a rare 1925 catalog, this architectural showcase features floor plans, construction details, and photos of 26 homes, plus articles on entrances, porches, garages, and more. 250 illustrations, 21 color plates. 176pp. 8⅜ x 11. 0-486-47028-8

MY 66 YEARS IN THE BIG LEAGUES, Connie Mack. With a New Introduction by Rich Westcott. A Founding Father of modern baseball, Mack holds the record for most wins — and losses — by a major league manager. Enhanced by 70 photographs, his warmhearted autobiography is populated by many legends of the game. 288pp. 5⅜ x 8½. 0-486-47184-5

NARRATIVE OF THE LIFE OF FREDERICK DOUGLASS, Frederick Douglass. Douglass's graphic depictions of slavery, harrowing escape to freedom, and life as a newspaper editor, eloquent orator, and impassioned abolitionist. 96pp. 5³⁄₁₆ x 8¼. 0-486-28499-9

THE NIGHTLESS CITY: Geisha and Courtesan Life in Old Tokyo, J. E. de Becker. This unsurpassed study from 100 years ago ventured into Tokyo's red-light district to survey geisha and courtesan life and offer meticulous descriptions of training, dress, social hierarchy, and erotic practices. 49 black-and-white illustrations; 2 maps. 496pp. 5⅜ x 8½. 0-486-45563-7

THE ODYSSEY, Homer. Excellent prose translation of ancient epic recounts adventures of the homeward-bound Odysseus. Fantastic cast of gods, giants, cannibals, sirens, other supernatural creatures — true classic of Western literature. 256pp. 5³⁄₁₆ x 8¼. 0-486-40654-7

OEDIPUS REX, Sophocles. Landmark of Western drama concerns the catastrophe that ensues when King Oedipus discovers he has inadvertently killed his father and married his mother. Masterly construction, dramatic irony. Explanatory footnotes. 64pp. 5³⁄₁₆ x 8¼. 0-486-26877-2

ONCE UPON A TIME: The Way America Was, Eric Sloane. Nostalgic text and drawings brim with gentle philosophies and descriptions of how we used to live — self-sufficiently — on the land, in homes, and among the things built by hand. 44 line illustrations. 64pp. 8⅜ x 11. 0-486-44411-2

ONE OF OURS, Willa Cather. The Pulitzer Prize–winning novel about a young Nebraskan looking for something to believe in. Alienated from his parents, rejected by his wife, he finds his destiny on the bloody battlefields of World War I. 352pp. $5\frac{3}{16}$ x $8\frac{1}{4}$. 0-486-45599-8

ORIGAMI YOU CAN USE: 27 Practical Projects, Rick Beech. Origami models can be more than decorative, and this unique volume shows how! The 27 practical projects include a CD case, frame, napkin ring, and dish. Easy instructions feature 400 two-color illustrations. 96pp. $8\frac{1}{4}$ x 11. 0-486-47057-1

OTHELLO, William Shakespeare. Towering tragedy tells the story of a Moorish general who earns the enmity of his ensign Iago when he passes him over for a promotion. Masterly portrait of an archvillain. Explanatory footnotes. 112pp. $5\frac{3}{16}$ x $8\frac{1}{4}$. 0-486-29097-2

PARADISE LOST, John Milton. Notes by John A. Himes. First published in 1667, *Paradise Lost* ranks among the greatest of English literature's epic poems. It's a sublime retelling of Adam and Eve's fall from grace and expulsion from Eden. Notes by John A. Himes. 480pp. $5\frac{3}{16}$ x $8\frac{1}{4}$. 0-486-44287-X

PASSING, Nella Larsen. Married to a successful physician and prominently ensconced in society, Irene Redfield leads a charmed existence — until a chance encounter with a childhood friend who has been "passing for white." 112pp. $5\frac{3}{8}$ x $8\frac{1}{2}$. 0-486-43713-2

PERSPECTIVE DRAWING FOR BEGINNERS, Len A. Doust. Doust carefully explains the roles of lines, boxes, and circles, and shows how visualizing shapes and forms can be used in accurate depictions of perspective. One of the most concise introductions available. 33 illustrations. 64pp. $5\frac{3}{8}$ x $8\frac{1}{2}$. 0-486-45149-6

PERSPECTIVE MADE EASY, Ernest R. Norling. Perspective is easy; yet, surprisingly few artists know the simple rules that make it so. Remedy that situation with this simple, step-by-step book, the first devoted entirely to the topic. 256 illustrations. 224pp. $5\frac{3}{8}$ x $8\frac{1}{2}$. 0-486-40473-0

THE PICTURE OF DORIAN GRAY, Oscar Wilde. Celebrated novel involves a handsome young Londoner who sinks into a life of depravity. His body retains perfect youth and vigor while his recent portrait reflects the ravages of his crime and sensuality. 176pp. $5\frac{3}{16}$ x $8\frac{1}{4}$. 0-486-27807-7

PRIDE AND PREJUDICE, Jane Austen. One of the most universally loved and admired English novels, an effervescent tale of rural romance transformed by Jane Austen's art into a witty, shrewdly observed satire of English country life. 272pp. $5\frac{3}{16}$ x $8\frac{1}{4}$. 0-486-28473-5

THE PRINCE, Niccolò Machiavelli. Classic, Renaissance-era guide to acquiring and maintaining political power. Today, nearly 500 years after it was written, this calculating prescription for autocratic rule continues to be much read and studied. 80pp. $5\frac{3}{16}$ x $8\frac{1}{4}$. 0-486-27274-5

QUICK SKETCHING, Carl Cheek. A perfect introduction to the technique of "quick sketching." Drawing upon an artist's immediate emotional responses, this is an extremely effective means of capturing the essential form and features of a subject. More than 100 black-and-white illustrations throughout. 48pp. 11 x $8\frac{1}{4}$. 0-486-46608-6

RANCH LIFE AND THE HUNTING TRAIL, Theodore Roosevelt. Illustrated by Frederic Remington. Beautifully illustrated by Remington, Roosevelt's celebration of the Old West recounts his adventures in the Dakota Badlands of the 1880s, from roundups to Indian encounters to hunting bighorn sheep. 208pp. $6\frac{1}{4}$ x $9\frac{1}{4}$. 0-486-47340-6

THE RED BADGE OF COURAGE, Stephen Crane. Amid the nightmarish chaos of a Civil War battle, a young soldier discovers courage, humility, and, perhaps, wisdom. Uncanny re-creation of actual combat. Enduring landmark of American fiction. 112pp. 5³⁄₁₆ x 8¼. 0-486-26465-3

RELATIVITY SIMPLY EXPLAINED, Martin Gardner. One of the subject's clearest, most entertaining introductions offers lucid explanations of special and general theories of relativity, gravity, and spacetime, models of the universe, and more. 100 illustrations. 224pp. 5⅜ x 8½. 0-486-29315-7

REMBRANDT DRAWINGS: 116 Masterpieces in Original Color, Rembrandt van Rijn. This deluxe hardcover edition features drawings from throughout the Dutch master's prolific career. Informative captions accompany these beautifully reproduced landscapes, biblical vignettes, figure studies, animal sketches, and portraits. 128pp. 8⅜ x 11. 0-486-46149-1

THE ROAD NOT TAKEN AND OTHER POEMS, Robert Frost. A treasury of Frost's most expressive verse. In addition to the title poem: "An Old Man's Winter Night," "In the Home Stretch," "Meeting and Passing," "Putting in the Seed," many more. All complete and unabridged. 64pp. 5³⁄₁₆ x 8¼. 0-486-27550-7

ROMEO AND JULIET, William Shakespeare. Tragic tale of star-crossed lovers, feuding families and timeless passion contains some of Shakespeare's most beautiful and lyrical love poetry. Complete, unabridged text with explanatory footnotes. 96pp. 5³⁄₁₆ x 8¼. 0-486-27557-4

SANDITON AND THE WATSONS: Austen's Unfinished Novels, Jane Austen. Two tantalizing incomplete stories revisit Austen's customary milieu of courtship and venture into new territory, amid guests at a seaside resort. Both are worth reading for pleasure and study. 112pp. 5⅜ x 8½. 0-486-45793-1

THE SCARLET LETTER, Nathaniel Hawthorne. With stark power and emotional depth, Hawthorne's masterpiece explores sin, guilt, and redemption in a story of adultery in the early days of the Massachusetts Colony. 192pp. 5³⁄₁₆ x 8¼.
0-486-28048-9

THE SEASONS OF AMERICA PAST, Eric Sloane. Seventy-five illustrations depict cider mills and presses, sleds, pumps, stump-pulling equipment, plows, and other elements of America's rural heritage. A section of old recipes and household hints adds additional color. 160pp. 8⅜ x 11. 0-486-44220-9

SELECTED CANTERBURY TALES, Geoffrey Chaucer. Delightful collection includes the General Prologue plus three of the most popular tales: "The Knight's Tale," "The Miller's Prologue and Tale," and "The Wife of Bath's Prologue and Tale." In modern English. 144pp. 5³⁄₁₆ x 8¼. 0-486-28241-4

SELECTED POEMS, Emily Dickinson. Over 100 best-known, best-loved poems by one of America's foremost poets, reprinted from authoritative early editions. No comparable edition at this price. Index of first lines. 64pp. 5³⁄₁₆ x 8¼. 0-486-26466-1

SIDDHARTHA, Hermann Hesse. Classic novel that has inspired generations of seekers. Blending Eastern mysticism and psychoanalysis, Hesse presents a strikingly original view of man and culture and the arduous process of self-discovery, reconciliation, harmony, and peace. 112pp. 5³⁄₁₆ x 8¼. 0-486-40653-9

SKETCHING OUTDOORS, Leonard Richmond. This guide offers beginners step-by-step demonstrations of how to depict clouds, trees, buildings, and other outdoor sights. Explanations of a variety of techniques include shading and constructional drawing. 48pp. 11 x 8¼. 0-486-46922-0

Browse over 9,000 books at www.doverpublications.com

SMALL HOUSES OF THE FORTIES: With Illustrations and Floor Plans, Harold E. Group. 56 floor plans and elevations of houses that originally cost less than $15,000 to build. Recommended by financial institutions of the era, they range from Colonials to Cape Cods. 144pp. 8⅜ x 11. 0-486-45598-X

SOME CHINESE GHOSTS, Lafcadio Hearn. Rooted in ancient Chinese legends, these richly atmospheric supernatural tales are recounted by an expert in Oriental lore. Their originality, power, and literary charm will captivate readers of all ages. 96pp. 5⅜ x 8½. 0-486-46306-0

SONGS FOR THE OPEN ROAD: Poems of Travel and Adventure, Edited by The American Poetry & Literacy Project. More than 80 poems by 50 American and British masters celebrate real and metaphorical journeys. Poems by Whitman, Byron, Millay, Sandburg, Langston Hughes, Emily Dickinson, Robert Frost, Shelley, Tennyson, Yeats, many others. Note. 80pp. 5³⁄₁₆ x 8¼. 0-486-40646-6

SPOON RIVER ANTHOLOGY, Edgar Lee Masters. An American poetry classic, in which former citizens of a mythical midwestern town speak touchingly from the grave of the thwarted hopes and dreams of their lives. 144pp. 5³⁄₁₆ x 8¼.
0-486-27275-3

STAR LORE: Myths, Legends, and Facts, William Tyler Olcott. Captivating retellings of the origins and histories of ancient star groups include Pegasus, Ursa Major, Pleiades, signs of the zodiac, and other constellations. "Classic." — *Sky & Telescope.* 58 illustrations. 544pp. 5⅜ x 8½. 0-486-43581-4

THE STRANGE CASE OF DR. JEKYLL AND MR. HYDE, Robert Louis Stevenson. This intriguing novel, both fantasy thriller and moral allegory, depicts the struggle of two opposing personalities — one essentially good, the other evil — for the soul of one man. 64pp. 5³⁄₁₆ x 8¼. 0-486-26688-5

SURVIVAL HANDBOOK: The Official U.S. Army Guide, Department of the Army. This special edition of the Army field manual is geared toward civilians. An essential companion for campers and all lovers of the outdoors, it constitutes the most authoritative wilderness guide. 288pp. 5³⁄₁₆ x 8¼. 0-486-46184-X

A TALE OF TWO CITIES, Charles Dickens. Against the backdrop of the French Revolution, Dickens unfolds his masterpiece of drama, adventure, and romance about a man falsely accused of treason. Excitement and derring-do in the shadow of the guillotine. 304pp. 5³⁄₁₆ x 8¼. 0-486-40651-2

TEN PLAYS, Anton Chekhov. *The Sea Gull, Uncle Vanya, The Three Sisters, The Cherry Orchard,* and *Ivanov,* plus 5 one-act comedies: *The Anniversary, An Unwilling Martyr, The Wedding, The Bear,* and *The Proposal.* 336pp. 5³⁄₁₆ x 8¼. 0-486-46560-8

THE FLYING INN, G. K. Chesterton. Hilarious romp in which pub owner Humphrey Hump and friend take to the road in a donkey cart filled with rum and cheese, inveighing against Prohibition and other "oppressive forms of modernity." 320pp. 5⅜ x 8½. 0-486-41910-X

THIRTY YEARS THAT SHOOK PHYSICS: The Story of Quantum Theory, George Gamow. Lucid, accessible introduction to the influential theory of energy and matter features careful explanations of Dirac's anti-particles, Bohr's model of the atom, and much more. Numerous drawings. 1966 edition. 240pp. 5⅜ x 8½. 0-486-24895-X

TREASURE ISLAND, Robert Louis Stevenson. Classic adventure story of a perilous sea journey, a mutiny led by the infamous Long John Silver, and a lethal scramble for buried treasure — seen through the eyes of cabin boy Jim Hawkins. 160pp. 5³⁄₁₆ x 8¼.
0-486-27559-0

Browse over 9,000 books at www.doverpublications.com

THE TRIAL, Franz Kafka. Translated by David Wyllie. From its gripping first sentence onward, this novel exemplifies the term "Kafkaesque." Its darkly humorous narrative recounts a bank clerk's entrapment in a bureaucratic maze, based on an undisclosed charge. 176pp. 5³⁄₁₆ x 8¼.   0-486-47061-X

THE TURN OF THE SCREW, Henry James. Gripping ghost story by great novelist depicts the sinister transformation of 2 innocent children into flagrant liars and hypocrites. An elegantly told tale of unspoken horror and psychological terror. 96pp. 5³⁄₁₆ x 8¼.   0-486-26684-2

UP FROM SLAVERY, Booker T. Washington. Washington (1856-1915) rose to become the most influential spokesman for African-Americans of his day. In this eloquently written book, he describes events in a remarkable life that began in bondage and culminated in worldwide recognition. 160pp. 5³⁄₁₆ x 8¼.   0-486-28738-6

VICTORIAN HOUSE DESIGNS IN AUTHENTIC FULL COLOR: 75 Plates from the "Scientific American – Architects and Builders Edition," 1885-1894, Edited by Blanche Cirker. Exquisitely detailed, exceptionally handsome designs for an enormous variety of attractive city dwellings, spacious suburban and country homes, charming "cottages" and other structures — all accompanied by perspective views and floor plans. 80pp. 9¼ x 12¼.   0-486-29438-2

VILLETTE, Charlotte Brontë. Acclaimed by Virginia Woolf as "Brontë's finest novel," this moving psychological study features a remarkably modern heroine who abandons her native England for a new life as a schoolteacher in Belgium. 480pp. 5³⁄₁₆ x 8¼.   0-486-45557-2

THE VOYAGE OUT, Virginia Woolf. A moving depiction of the thrills and confusion of youth, Woolf's acclaimed first novel traces a shipboard journey to South America for a captivating exploration of a woman's growing self-awareness. 288pp. 5³⁄₁₆ x 8¼.   0-486-45005-8

WALDEN; OR, LIFE IN THE WOODS, Henry David Thoreau. Accounts of Thoreau's daily life on the shores of Walden Pond outside Concord, Massachusetts, are interwoven with musings on the virtues of self-reliance and individual freedom, on society, government, and other topics. 224pp. 5³⁄₁₆ x 8¼.   0-486-28495-6

WILD PILGRIMAGE: A Novel in Woodcuts, Lynd Ward. Through startling engravings shaded in black and red, Ward wordlessly tells the story of a man trapped in an industrial world, struggling between the grim reality around him and the fantasies his imagination creates. 112pp. 6⅛ x 9¼.   0-486-46583-7

WILLY POGÁNY REDISCOVERED, Willy Pogány. Selected and Edited by Jeff A. Menges. More than 100 color and black-and-white Art Nouveau–style illustrations from fairy tales and adventure stories include scenes from Wagner's "Ring" cycle, *The Rime of the Ancient Mariner, Gulliver's Travels,* and *Faust.* 144pp. 8⅜ x 11.
                          0-486-47046-6

WOOLLY THOUGHTS: Unlock Your Creative Genius with Modular Knitting, Pat Ashforth and Steve Plummer. Here's the revolutionary way to knit — easy, fun, and foolproof! Beginners and experienced knitters need only master a single stitch to create their own designs with patchwork squares. More than 100 illustrations. 128pp. 6½ x 9¼.   0-486-46084-3

WUTHERING HEIGHTS, Emily Brontë. Somber tale of consuming passions and vengeance — played out amid the lonely English moors — recounts the turbulent and tempestuous love story of Cathy and Heathcliff. Poignant and compelling. 256pp. 5³⁄₁₆ x 8¼.   0-486-29256-8